BITCC

BLOCKCHAIN

BASICS

A non-technical introduction for beginners on Bitcoin, Blockchain Technology, Cryptocurrency, Altcoins, Ethereum, Ripple, Investing, Mining, Wallets, Trading, Law, Smart Contracts, ICO, IOT and Digital Currency.

Arthur T. Brooks

Contents

Introduction

Bitcoin and the blockchain continue to make headline news and social media streams are continually reporting on the current status of the mysterious crypto world. The perceived high risk, high reward and volatile nature of digital currency and the blockchain that supports it continues to intrigue both potential investors and consumers. Its popularity is growing by the day however one basic problem remains- most people still don't really know what it is or how they can benefit from it.

It's no surprise that people are confused. On the face of it, bitcoin and blockchain appear to be complicated and highly technical subjects which you will have zero chance of understanding at all, unless you happen to be a techno whiz with a master's degree in Programming or Computer Science. Some people still think that it's a scam while others firmly believe that it is poised to completely revolutionize the way we make transactions. Whatever your view, cryptocurrency it is here to stay, and the fact is that every single one of us can get involved if we choose.

In truth, all you really need to get started is no nonsense, jargon free and easy to digest information and that is exactly why this book was written. It is specifically structured so that the average person (like me) who has no relevant prior knowledge whatsoever can finally understand everything that they need to know to enter the world of cryptocurrency and blockchain with complete confidence.

What you learn in this book will change the way that you think about money and you will be able to make an actionable plan to fully take advantage of what virtual currency has to offer.

We have a lot to discuss. Are you ready? I'm ready. Let's get started right now.

-Please consider taking a moment to leave an honest review-

Should You Invest in Crypto?

It's a big question. Cryptocurrencies seem to be taking over the world. Many people are starting to hear about them and are interested in learning whether these are going to be the answer that they are looking for in order to finally make some money. However, with all the hype that has come out about these digital currencies, you may be curious about whether these are really that good of an investment to choose, or if you should go with another investment option. Some cryptocurrencies are going to be great investments, while others may just ride out the popularity and hope they succeed.

What exactly are Cryptocurrencies?

A cryptocurrency is a digital or virtual currency, one that often works like fiat money as a medium of exchange. While fiat currencies rely on a government agency to help keep them running, these cryptocurrencies will rely on cryptography to keep them secure, help to verify transactions, and to basically keep them running. Also, this same cryptography is going to be used to help create some new units of a cryptocurrency.

You can use these currencies in a similar way to how you normally use fiat money for all your online transactions. As of right now, you are not able to use these currencies offline, meaning that it is not possible to print off paper versions of these currencies and then take them shopping with you. But, for those who like to shop online, those who want to invest, or those who need to send money to others no matter where they live throughout the world, these cryptocurrencies can help make it all happen.

To help you understand more about cryptocurrencies and how they work, let's examine the differences between these cryptocurrencies and the fiat money you are used to. When we talk about fiat money, we are talking about the traditional money used in your country of origin. This is the money that you can go to the bank and get, the money that you can use to pay your bills or use at the grocery store.

This currency is considered valuable because the government is there to back it up. If the government, or another big agency in your country, took away their backing, the currency would become worthless. If something does go wrong in concerns to the currency, such as your bank going under, the government will be there to provide you with your funds, rather than you losing all your money.

Fiat currency is the currency that most people rely on. They like it when someone else can control the money, and that 'someone' is there to guarantee that the money will be worth something each day. However, there are some people who wish the government would stay out of their transactions. They may feel that the government is not able to do a good job of controlling the money, or that the government has no business sticking their nose into their money. Many don't trust the government after all the issues that occurred with the economic downturn of 2008. These people would rather oversee their own money rather than letting the government take over it.

This is where cryptocurrency comes into play. On the surface, cryptocurrencies are going to work in a similar manner as fiat currencies in that you can use this online currency to make purchases. You can also send money to people in other countries and accept the currency as payment for your own goods or services. One noticeable difference though is that this is a currency that will only work online. You will never be able to print off this currency to use at a regular store, and there are a limited number of online retailers who will accept cryptocurrencies at this time.

The biggest difference in fiat currency and cryptocurrencies is that with cryptocurrencies, there are no central agencies that run the currency. You will not find any bank or government who runs the currency. Instead, they rely on mathematical equations and the Blockchain Technology to help it run. For many users, this is a benefit that helps them to complete the transactions that they want in a secure way.

These mathematical equations are challenging, which are meant to ensure the market keeps going without needing someone to come in and make changes. This can be a nice change to those who would like to keep their privacy when making purchases or performing other things online.

Why are cryptocurrencies good investment options?

Many people are considering using these cryptocurrencies to make money. They see that there is much potential out there for these currencies and for them to make money in the process. In fact, many of those who join these networks not only use them to invest in the blockchain or to send and receive payments, but also as a form of investing. And since many of these coins are expected to continue rising in the future, it looks like a very lucrative investment vehicle.

There are a few things to watch out for here to ensure that you understand how to work with cryptocurrency investment:

First, clearly if you just jump into this investment because you hear someone else say that they are good investments, you will fail. There are more than 1000 cryptocurrencies out there right now, but most of them are going to fail. However, with a bit of research, you are likely to figure out which ones will fail before you even jump in.

The problem is that some people want to get into the market right away, and they are attracted to the coins that cost little to join. But if you spend $1000 on a currency that never takes off, it really doesn't matter how many coins you got for that money; you will still lose that initial investment.

If you want to get into the cryptocurrency market to invest, then you must be able to do your own up to date research. You need to know which currencies are likely to take off and why, and you must be able to read the market and understand when a coin will go up or down in value. Starting with a coin that costs less money can be a great way to earn considerable profit. For example, when Bitcoin started, it was $1 for 1 Bitcoin in 2009. By 2017, the value had risen to $20,000. That is a huge amount of profit that you can earn.

But not all coins are going to be like Bitcoin. Even if you get the coins for a good deal, if they fail, you could lose. It is essential to look at the structure that is behind each coin that you want to consider and see whether it has the potential to do well.

Another thing to consider is the timing of the market. Many people want to jump onto Bitcoin because it is big and powerful and seems like it will make them money. But even Bitcoin has had some major downturns. Remember back in December of 2017, the value of Bitcoin reached almost $20,000. But by January of 2018, the amount had fallen, almost overnight, to under $10,000 and reached much lower than that before it levelled out and started slowly going up again.

If you had purchased some coins about nine to ten months before December of 2017, you could have bought them for around $2500 and then sold them in December for a profit. However, if you purchased the coins in December when they were at an all-time high, then you would have lost all that money when the downturn hit.

Therefore it is so important to learn how to read the market and be prepared. Many people lost fortunes in this market because they jumped on Bitcoin too late in the game. If you are just going to follow the crowd and are not willing to wait a bit to earn a profit, then investing in cryptocurrency is not the best idea for you.

And finally, you must consider what each coin does. Not all coins are used for transactions like Bitcoin is. If you pick out a currency thinking that it works just like Bitcoin, and it doesn't, then you really do not know what you are investing in. For example, Bitcoin is a peer-to-peer payment system. Ethereum is a way to develop the 'blockchain technology', and Ripple is an exchange site to send money to people all around the world in various currencies, both fiat, and crypto. None of them is going to behave in the same manner, and it is important to realise this before investing in them.

This is not to turn you away from investing in cryptocurrencies. There are many people who enjoy investing in these currencies and who have made a lot of money. You could do the same. But this is not a get rich quick scheme and it is not without risks. You must treat it just like you would any other investment you start. If you take your time, are willing to wait out the ups and downs, and are eager to do your own research, you will find that cryptocurrency can be the best investment tool for your needs.

Which are the best cryptocurrencies?

If you are interested in getting started with investing in cryptocurrencies, there are many options to go with. These have gained so much popularity that there are now over 1000 of these coins on the market to choose from, but how are you supposed to know which one the best option for your needs is? Some of the best cryptocurrencies that you can choose from include:

- **Bitcoin:** Most people who have heard about cryptocurrencies have most likely heard about Bitcoin. This is the first cryptocurrency on the market, and it is considered a peer-to-peer payment system. You are only able to use the coins that you get on this network online, but if you like to invest or like to shop online already, you probably won't see some big differences between working with a credit card or working with Bitcoin. This is a platform that uses the blockchain, and you will be able to send as well as receive money from anywhere in the world in real time and without high transaction fees.

- **Ethereum:** Right behind Bitcoin is Ethereum. This one works slightly different than what you see with Bitcoin because it concentrates more on expanding out what the blockchain technology can do rather than focusing on sending and receiving money. Those who go onto this network will be able to use the open-sourced blockchain that is available there to create their very own application of the blockchain. When you are on the Ethereum network, you will be able to use the Ether coin to help pay for fees and other things that are needed to develop your own blockchain application.

- **Ripple:** Another option that you can use when going with a cryptocurrency to invest in is Ripple. This is a platform that will help you to send money to others, no matter where they may be, and you can even use traditional currencies. It works with Ethereum, Bitcoin, Litecoin, USD, Euro, and so many more. Ripple is set up to take on any currency and then move it to someone else in the world almost instantly. While it is sometimes used by individuals to send money to each other, most of the time it is used by larger enterprises.

- **Litecoin:** Litecoin works in a similar manner to Bitcoin in that it is a peer-to-peer payment system. However, it has been updated and changed a bit in order to make it easier to use and to get rid of some of the bugs that have come with the Bitcoin network. For example, with the Litecoin network, you are able to get the transaction done in two and a half minutes, compared to Bitcoin that can take ten minutes. There are also more coins available on the Litecoin network compared to the Bitcoin, to help it run better.

- **Dogecoin:** And finally, you may want to consider working with Dogecoin. It has another option to help you out because it is different from the others. This is a currency that you use to tip people on either their website or their social media sites. When you go through some content and you like what you see, you will be able to send some of these coins over to tip them. Right now, these are new and may not have a lot of value, which is why they are used mostly to tip someone rather than one of the major contenders or a payment option at this time.

These are just a few of the options that you can choose from when you are looking to invest in a cryptocurrency for your own needs. It really depends on what you are looking for when it comes to investing. For example, Bitcoin may be more secure and have a high value, but this makes it hard to enter the market because the price is so high. You need to look at all the different types of currencies, do your research, and pick out the right cryptocurrency that works for you.

How can I store my cryptocurrency?

Unlike fiat currency, you are not able to print off these currencies and store in your physical wallet and then use them how you want. So, how are you supposed to use these currencies to make payments?

There are online wallets that you can use that will store these currencies for you. There are many different options that you can choose from based on the features that you want and how much security is necessary.

If you sign up with an exchange site, you will receive an online wallet from the site. This option works well if you plan to use the currencies right away. If you plan on investing those coins, it is better to pick out one of the other types of wallets to keep the coins more secure.

There are a few types of wallets that you can use for this. Some of the different wallet types that you can choose from include:

- Online wallet: Best if you plan to use the coins right away.
- Hardware wallet: If you would like to store the coins for some time but do not want them to be too far from the online wallet for easy use.
- Cold storage: Best for long-term storage where you want to ensure that no one is able to get access to the coins and take them away from you.

We will spend more time talking about each of these wallets later; nevertheless, they are so important for helping you to keep your coins safe and ensuring that a hacker is not able to get onto the network and steal all your money.

Does anyone accept these coins?

Before you get into a new investment opportunity, you want to make sure that it has a solid base that will help it to grow and earn you money. One way to figure out how well these cryptocurrencies will do is whether they are accepted by various businesses and companies online. The bigger the companies who accept these, the more likely that the coin will gain in value.

Cryptocurrencies are relatively new. Because of this, the list of retailers that accept these coins as a form of payment is not as much as some users may like. With that being said, there are still a number of places that will take these coins, and some of them are major retailers.

Bitcoin is one of the most widely accepted cryptocurrencies out there. The list of companies that currently accept Bitcoin is increasing, and it is going to grow into the future. These retailers include both in-store and online stores. All companies accepting Bitcoin and other cryptocurrencies will include a payment button on their website (and they usually advertise this fact), so it is easy for you to see it right away.

In some cases, you may find that there are some local companies that will accept Bitcoin in their stores. Using your Bitcoin, even though you can't print off paper versions of the coin, is easy. You just need to add an app to your smartphone that will provide you with a barcode. Inside this barcode, you will have information on your private key. The company will simply need to scan the barcode, and the coins will be transferred.

The bad news is that the list of companies, especially major companies that accept these coins is still small. The good news is that as more people start to use these currencies, and the more prevalent these currencies become, the more likely it is that companies will start joining this list.

Bitcoin Explained

Bitcoin is digital money that is not issued or controlled by anyone. It is used to securely store and transfer any amount of value anywhere in the world. It is used to buy goods and services, store wealth, or send value to anyone without the permission of a third party. Often regarded as "Digital Gold," bitcoin that is stored properly cannot be hacked, stolen or seized by a government — thus giving people full proprietorship much like having a Swiss bank account in their pocket. Unlike physical gold, Bitcoin is cheaper, faster, and more efficient to store or send anywhere in the world. Bitcoin is divisible to the eighth decimal place and is completely digital, allowing the transfer of any monetary value. Opposed to government "fiat" currencies, which can be manipulated and devalued, there is a finite supply of 21 million bitcoins, making it a scarce and valuable asset. Bitcoin is the internet of money and will do to finance what the internet did for communication.

Why Bitcoin?

Bitcoins can be used to buy merchandise anonymously. Also, international payments are easy and cheap because bitcoins are not tied to any country or subject to regulation. Small businesses may like them because there are no credit card fees. Some people buy bitcoins as an investment, hoping that they'll go up in value.

How Does it Work?

The Bitcoin network is a peer-to-peer network that runs on a decentralized distributed self-clearing ledger called the blockchain. Units of currency that run on the Bitcoin network are called bitcoins, which are used to store and transmit value among network participants. Unlike most currencies issued by central banks, which can be devalued and manipulated, bitcoins are issued according to a fixed set of rules to create sound money that can't be manipulated by a central authority or malicious actor. Users can buy or sell goods and services, send money to people or organizations, or even extend credit in a fast, secure, and borderless manner. The only prerequisite for access to these coins is an internet connection and a private key that forms a pair with public-facing keys to provide access to the coins stored on the Bitcoin network. Unauthorized access to someone's private key is analogous to stealing gold from their vault.

The Basics for a New User

As a new user, you can get started with Bitcoin without understanding the technical details. Once you have installed a Bitcoin wallet on your computer or mobile phone, it will generate your first Bitcoin address, and you can create more whenever you need one. You can disclose your addresses to your friends so that they can pay you or vice versa. This is pretty similar to how email works, except that Bitcoin addresses should only be used once.

Balances – Blockchain

The blockchain is a shared public ledger on which the entire Bitcoin network relies. All confirmed transactions are included in the blockchain. This way, Bitcoin wallets can calculate their spendable balance, and new transactions can be verified to be spending bitcoins that are owned by the spender. The integrity and the chronological order of the blockchain are enforced with cryptography. More on blockchain later.

Transactions - Private Keys

A transaction is a transfer of value between Bitcoin wallets that gets included in the blockchain. Bitcoin wallets keep a secret piece of data called a private key or seed, which is used to sign transactions, providing a mathematical proof that they have come from the owner of the wallet. The signature also prevents the transaction from being altered by anybody once it has been issued. All transactions are broadcast between users and usually begin to be confirmed by the network in the following 10 minutes, through a process called mining.

Processing - Mining

Mining is a distributed consensus system that is used to confirm waiting transactions by including them in the blockchain. It enforces a chronological order in the blockchain, protects the neutrality of the network, and allows different computers to agree on the state of the system. To be confirmed, transactions must be packed in a block that fits stringent cryptographic rules that will be verified by the network. These rules prevent previous blocks from being modified because doing so would invalidate all following blocks. Mining also creates the equivalent of a competitive lottery that prevents any individual from easily adding new blocks consecutively in the blockchain. This way, no individuals can control what is included in the blockchain or replace parts of the block chain to roll back their spends.

Benefits of Bitcoin

Most people have heard of the term Bitcoin but don't have a clear idea of what it is. As per the definition, Bitcoin is a decentralized, peer to peer, digital currency system, designed to give online users the ability to process transactions via digital unit of exchange known as Bitcoins. In other words, it is a virtual currency.

A private network of computers connected by a shared program is used to carry out transactions and process payments in Bitcoin. The creation of Bitcoins are based on increasingly complex mathematical algorithms, and its purchase is made with standard national money currencies. Users of Bitcoin can access their coins with their smartphones or computers.

As a new and growing virtual currency, Bitcoin has certain distinct advantages over the conventional government flat currencies. **Here are some of the benefits that you will enjoy when using Bitcoin:**

One of the benefits of Bitcoin is its low inflation risk. Traditional currencies suffer from inflation, and they tend to lose their purchasing power each year, as governments continue to use quantitative easing to stimulate the economy.

Bitcoin doesn't suffer from low inflation because Bitcoin mining is limited to just 21 million units. That means the release of new Bitcoins is slowing down and the full amount will be mined out within the next couple of decades. Experts have predicted that the last Bitcoin will be mined by 2050.

Bitcoin has a low risk of collapse, unlike traditional currencies that rely on governments. When currencies collapse, it leads to hyperinflation or the wipeout of one's savings in an instant.

Bitcoin exchange rate is not regulated by any government and is a digital currency available worldwide.

- **Bitcoin is easy to carry.**

A billion dollars in the Bitcoin can be stored on a memory stick and placed in one's pocket. It is easy to transport Bitcoins compared to paper money.

- **Bitcoin has a minimal transaction fees.**

Fees and exchange costs are part and parcel of standard wire transfers and international purchases. Bitcoin is not monitored or moderated by any intermediary institution or government agency. Therefore, the costs of transacting are kept very low, unlike international transactions made via conventional currencies.

When making a Bitcoin transfer, the fees are low compared to conventional methods of moving money. A normal Bitcoin fee is 0.0005 BTC per transfer, whereas with a typically international wire transfer you could expect to pay 700THB-1300THB per transaction. Accepting credit cards will generally cost 3-5% of the transfer amount, which again is much more expensive than a Bitcoin transaction.

In addition to this, transactions in Bitcoin are not known to be time-consuming since it does not involve the complications of typical authorization reⓠuirements and waiting periods.

- **Bitcoin has an appreciating value.**

The value of Bitcoins was initially highly volatile during the first few years of its inception, however, in more recent times, the currency has stabilized and has been steadily increasing in value daily.

- **Bitcoin has a safer ecosystem.**

An authentic digital signature signs each bitcoin wallet transaction before it is sent to a blockchain.

This complete process makes the app a safe place for storing and exchanging cryptocurrencies.

- **International payments made easy for small business ventures.**

Small online sellers and retailers don't often sell their services or products internationally because of the high cross-border transaction fees.

Bitcoins, being global, relives this pressure once and for all, thereby making payments cheaper, safer, easier, and faster.

- **No involvement of any third party.**

The entire process of bitcoin transactions is peer to peer. There's no involvement of a third party. No one can freeze, tax, or claim your coins. They cannot be stolen and cannot be seized by the Government in no possible circumstances.

- **Quick payments.**

Credit card funds can be locked up for as long as a week (or even more) in case a customer asks for a chargeback. Thus, payment delays occur for no reason whatsoever.

This is generally not the case with bitcoins. They are usually much quicker in comparison to conventional credit card settlements.

- **Easy to use in any situation.**

The international transportation of bitcoins is easy. All you will need is a simple memory stick, and you are sorted enough for the job.

You can even use the same currency in a different country without going through the pains of contacting the local bank for any purpose of currency conversions.

- **No-risk of inflation; individuals can preserve coins.**

With bitcoins, there are zero risks of inflation. Inflation usually occurs when the Government issues more money over the year, decreasing the purchasing power of the people, on the whole.

But the bitcoin system was created with the sole purpose of being finite (and that number is speculated to be around 21 million). Thus, without the possibilities of issuing excess currency, the threat of inflation comes down to almost zero. This point benefits both the seller and the buyer, in general.

- **Bitcoin can't be banned.**

Due to the nature of Bitcoin, there is constant talk about "banning" it. This hostility towards Bitcoin is because it works outside the jurisdiction of the traditional banking system.

However, the fundamental design is such that it can't be banned, only regulated. As long as you have an internet connection and a Bitcoin wallet, you can engage in Bitcoin.

Nevertheless, many countries have tried to ban it, like Bangladesh, Bolivia, Thailand, and Vietnam (among many others). But there are some countries including Australia, Russia, Japan, and Venezuela which have made Bitcoin an official legal tender and are regulating it.

However, some countries like India and even the USA are unclear about their official policy regarding cryptocurrencies. Try as they might, Bitcoin can't be pushed away just because it threatens the financial power structure. This is the real beauty of Bitcoin.

- **Bitcoin is not anonymous.**

Some effort is required to protect your privacy with Bitcoin. All Bitcoin transactions are stored publicly and permanently on the network, which means anyone can see the balance and transactions of any Bitcoin address. However, the identity of the user behind an address remains unknown until information is revealed during a purchase or in other circumstances. This is one reason why Bitcoin addresses should only be used once. Always remember that it is your responsibility to adopt good practices to protect your privacy.

- **No taxation.**

When you make purchases via dollars, euros, or any other government fiat currency, you have to pay an additional sum of money to the government as tax. Every purchasable item has its own designated tax rate. However, when you're purchasing Bitcoin, sales taxes are not added to your purchase. This is deemed as a legal form of tax evasion and is one of the major advantages of being a Bitcoin user.

With zero tax rates, Bitcoin can come in handy, especially when purchasing luxury items that are exclusive to a foreign land. Such items, more often than not, are heavily taxed by the Government.

How Can My Business Start Accepting Bitcoin from Customers?

If you run a small business and want to attract more customers by offering bitcoin payments, you may be wondering where to start. Keep in mind that it's not a way of avoiding taxes! Bitcoin is simply another legal way to receive payment for goods and services. So, you'll have to declare the payments as you would with traditional ones.

Businesses around the world are discovering that it pays to develop and employ a Bitcoin strategy. Bitcoin is easy to use; it provides fast transactions with lower costs than credit cards, as well as other benefits. Simply announcing "Bitcoin accepted here" brings with it news and social media attention. Bitcoin users will also go out of their way to support a Bitcoin business.

Because it offers fast, reliable, and cost-effective global transactions, we recommend accepting payments in Bitcoin Cash (BCH) on other digital currencies, such as Bitcoin Core (BTC). That's why this guide is focused specifically on BCH payments for businesses.

Accepting Bitcoin Cash (BCH) for eCommerce

- When your customers come to pay on your eCommerce website, you can give them the option to pay with BCH.

- This is done using a Bitcoin Cash payment gateway that you add to your website, allowing you to accept customer BCH payments.

- The payment gateway automatically calculates the amount due from BCH for items in your customer's shopping cart.

- Instead of asking them to enter the credit card information for the payment, they see a QR code (generated by the payment gateway) that they will easily scan with their digital wallet application.

An example of a payment gateway is called Bitpay. This will appear on your website so that customers can scan with their wallet app.

Explore payment gateways

Accept Bitcoin Cash (BCH) for in-store payments.

- Whether it's a restaurant, a cafeteria or a shop, you can offer your customers the opportunity to pay with BCH with their existing devices (tablets, smartphones, for example).

- Instead of paying in cash or by credit card, you use a point-of-sale application to accept payment at BCH.

- The app is downloaded to your device, and when customers are willing to pay, enter the amount due (in your local currency) into the app.

- The POS application automatically calculates the amount owed from BCH, and a QR code is generated on the screen of your device.

- Finally, show this QR code to the customer, who scans it with your wallet application.

Explore Point of Sale Apps

When will I receive the payment?

- Because Bitcoin Cash transactions do not have to go through slow payment processors, BCH payments are much faster than traditional payment methods.

- If you have chosen to receive BCH payments on your digital wallet, you will have that money with you in a few seconds.

- Or, if you choose to convert the BCH into the chosen currency first, the money is usually deposited into your commercial bank account the next business day.

How do I exchange Bitcoin payments into my local currency?

Through your payment gateway or your point-of-sale application

- If you prefer your customers' BCH payments to be automatically converted to your local currency before receiving them, you can do so.

- Easily choose a payment gateway (online company) or point of sale application (store company) offering this service, such as Bitpay.

- The service provider will receive the BCH paid for by their customers, and then deposits the equivalent amount of the chosen currency into their commercial bank account, usually the next business day.

- A small fee for this service will be deducted from the payment before you receive it.

Through a cryptocurrency exchange

- If you use a payment gateway or point-of-sale application that sends your customers' BCH payments directly to your digital wallet, you can convert them yourself via a reliable cryptocurrency exchange.

- You can exchange it for a fiduciary currency (for example, USD, GBP) or another cryptocurrency, such as Bitcoin Core (BTC) or Ethereum (ETH).

- To convert the BCH into your fiduciary currency, you must use an exchange that supports cryptographic currency trusts, such as Coinbase.

- Create an account and send the BCH of your digital wallet to the web wallet of your cryptocurrency exchange account.

- Follow the show instructions to sell your BCH via its platform.

- The exchange buys your BCH and sends the payment in the chosen currency to your bank account, minus the costs they charge for that service.

Through a trading platform

- You can also sell the BCH in your digital wallet via a peer-to-peer trading platform.

- Create an account and specify the amount of BCH you want to sell, as well as the type of payment you want to accept.

- This may include cash payments in person or online payments such as transfers.

- Send the BCH from your digital wallet to a secure blind deposit account, and as soon as you have received the buyer's agreed payment, the BCH is released and sent to your wallet.

- Rates are considerably lower on these trading platforms, which means you can keep more of your money.

How to Choose the Best Bitcoin Exchange

Bitcoin is not very different from a computer program or a mobile application that provides a personal wallet, allowing users to send and receive Bitcoins. Although there are many exchanges available for people seeking for an opportunity to trade or invest in BTC, knowledge on how the system works is critical before starting. The process of transferring money over an exchange can be rigorous. It is not easy to acquire, which explains why it is important to involve Bitcoin brokers or exchange. The process of finding a broker or exchange is more than finding one with the best-looking website. **The factors to consider when choosing an exchange include:**

- **Security**

Security is by far the most important factor of an exchange. If an exchange is insecure, your funds could be stolen, leaving any other advantages it offers worthless. No one wants to lose his or her money, so In this respect, consider the following aspects.

- **Technology**

  ✓ The exchange's web address should start with HTTPS. Avoid HTTP connections.
  ✓ For login safety, it should use two-factor authentication (username and password plus a piece of information only you have).
  ✓ Customer deposits should be stored offline in "cold storage."
  ✓ Auditing programs that monitor exchange activity 24/7 and SMS and email alerts all give exchange customers additional security guarantees.
  ✓ You may want to whitelist your IP address or withdrawal wallet addresses for the maximum security.

- **Payment Methods**

What payment methods are available on the exchange? Credit & debit card? Wire transfer? PayPal? If an exchange has limited payment options, then it may not be convenient for you to use it. Remember that purchasing cryptocurrencies with a credit card will always require identity verification and come with a premium price as there is a higher risk of fraud and higher transaction and processing fees. Purchasing cryptocurrency via wire transfer will take significantly longer as it takes time for banks to process.

- **Verification Requirements**

The vast majority of the Bitcoin trading platforms both in the US and the UK require some ID verification to make deposits & withdrawals. Some exchanges will allow you to remain anonymous. Although verification, which can take up to a few days, might seem like a pain, it protects the exchange against all kinds of scams and money laundering.

- **Legal aspects**

  ✓ It's recommended you use an exchange from the same country you are, as that can make it easier to comply with regulatory changes. It's also possible, though, to use other exchanges in other countries. Note that some exchanges support only a limited number of countries.
  ✓ Some exchanges may insure their funds, meaning that in case they lose your funds, you may be reimbursed.

- **Transparency**

  ✓ Does the exchange reveal its owners, headquarter address, and the members of its team?

✓ Transparent exchanges also publish their cold storage address or help check their reserves in other ways, like audit information.

In any case, don't leave your funds on any cryptocurrency exchange longer than necessary. Keep only the funds you need for trading. Most exchanges are like honeypots for hackers. Since they must keep many digital assets in one place, hackers create the most elaborate schemes to steal exchange user's funds. Hence, it's better to store the rest of your bitcoin in your private wallets.

- **Liquidity**

It is traded in a market where traders and investors are looking for an opportunity to sell or buy the currency. Therefore, it is advisable to consider the liquidity an exchange has. The term liquidity refers to the ability to sell an asset without the prices being affected significantly, in turn causing the prices to drop. When there are more sellers and buyers, the more the liquidity, some of the largest exchange offer high selling prices, which in turn creates an effect that allows the system to generate into a large network where more people can join.

- **Proximity**

Bitcoin remains relatively unregulated money, although the landscape is expected to change in the long-term. There is more exposure by financial industries and media in this regard. We will experience more governments wanting to exert some control over how monetary value is transmitted. This is attributed to the governments need to check and prevent the instrument from being used for illegal activities, such as money laundering, illegal drug smuggling, and terrorism. Because of the difference in prices, it is important to verify the geographic location of any exchange. Furthermore, the location of the exchange will dictate to investors and traders what laws they have to follow.

- **Fees**

Buying and selling do involve money. The money is ideally the incentive for the brokers or exchange. Nonetheless, unlike buying bonds or stocks, Bitcoin exchanges charge a percentage, while discount brokers used by most investors charge flat rate fees. The percentage model, purchasing, and selling over time can prove expensive. Some of the popular exchanges charge higher percentage fees based on a sliding scale, based on volume. Hence, they charge less percentage where more volumes have been traded within thirty days.

Different exchanges have different rates. You will be surprised how much you can save if you shop around. It's not uncommon for rates to fluctuate up to 10% and even higher in some instances.

- **User experience**

  - ✓ If you care about anonymity, you probably won't choose an exchange that requires you to reveal much about your identity;
  - ✓ Is the user interface simple and easy to use on both a desktop and a mobile device?
  - ✓ What do other users say about the benefits and drawbacks of a specific exchange, the support it offers, and so on? Check community forums like Bitcoin Reddit or Bitcoin Forum.

Types of exchanges

- **Trading Platforms:** These are websites that connect buyers and sellers and take a fee from each transaction.

- **Direct Trading:** These platforms offer direct person to person trading where individuals from different countries can exchange currency. Direct trading exchanges don't have a fixed market price. Instead, each seller sets their exchange rate.

- **Brokers:** These are websites that anyone can visit to buy cryptocurrencies at a price set by the broker. Bitcoin brokers are similar to foreign exchange dealers.

How to Buy Bitcoin Cash (BCH) with a Credit Card

Buying Bitcoin Cash (BCH) can seem complicated. But it doesn't have to be! This chapter will help you buy Bitcoin Cash directly with your credit/debit card. There are many different exchanges with different payment methods and fees. Some sites have a long and complicated process to buy Bitcoin Cash. Others charge expensive fees. It should be quick, easy, and cheap to buy Bitcoin Cash/BCH with a credit card!

This guide will show you a quick and easy way to buy Bitcoin Cash to get your bitcoins and be on your way to becoming an active participant in the Bitcoin economy.

Using a credit card to buy Bitcoin Cash

- **Create Account**

Buying Bitcoin Cash (BCH) is super simple by creating a Bitcoin Cash account with your information.

- **Verify Email & Sign In**

Next step is to verify your email to access your Bitcoin Cash account. Follow the email link, enter your information, and click on "Sign in."

- **Complete Profile**

First, let's remove the deposit limitation by answering some questions. (Don't worry, this is standard for all exchanges, and your private information is secure). Click on the button "Complete Profile" and follow their steps.

- **Make a Deposit**

Now it's time to make your deposit. Click on the button "Deposit Funds" and select the amount/payment method.

- **Select Bitcoin Cash**

Now you need to select Bitcoin Cash (BCH). Click on the buy button.

- **Buy Bitcoin Cash!**

The last step is to enter the amount and click on "Open Trade."

Once you have clicked on the buy button, you will be directed to the payment page where you will enter your details to finalize your purchase of Bitcoin Cash. Payments are usually processed within one hour; However, some cases require more attention, and approval may take up to 24 hours.

You will receive an email as soon as your payment has been verified. If your transaction is still pending, it may be because you have not yet submitted a verification request. In this case, an email will be sent to request proof of identity or ownership of the card, which could end up in your junk mail folder. If there is a delay, check your spam folder to see a verification email.

Before you can buy Bitcoin Cash, you'll need a Bitcoin Cash wallet to store it in. Hardware wallets that support Bitcoin Cash include industry leaders and TREZOR.

Both Ledger and TREZOR provide functions for you to use Bitcoin Cash as you would any other cryptocurrency. Both have also introduced the ability to claim your funds if you already owned Bitcoin at the time of the Bitcoin Cash hard fork.

Additionally, there are a variety of software wallets you can use to store Bitcoin Cash as well.

- Exodus provides a great user experience with a seamless coin exchange service known as Shapeshift built it.

- Edge is a mobile wallet for iOS and Android that supports multiple cryptocurrencies, including Bitcoin Cash. It also has a variety of features allowing you to buy cryptocurrencies and exchange them from within the app.

- Electron Cash is a clone of the awesome wallet for Bitcoin. If you're used to Electrum, then you'll have no problem jumping on board with its sister technology.

Other wallets that support BCH include Keepkey, BTC.com, Bitpay, and Coinomi.

Once you have your wallet, you will need your Bitcoin Cash address. It's a long string of letters and numbers that start with either a "1" or a "3" – similar to standard Bitcoin addresses.

Since many people got confused and started sending Bitcoins to Bitcoin Cash wallets and vice versa, a new format was invented for Bitcoin Cash. The format, called "Cash Address" is 42 characters long and starts with a "p" or a "⍰." **Here's an example:**

pm2sznhks23z7629mms6s4cwef74vcwvy22gdx6a

Keep in mind that Cash Addresses are just a representation of original Bitcoin Cash addresses. This means that the same address can be represented in two different ways (normal format or Cash Address format).

Not all wallets support Cash address format.

Find a Bitcoin Cash Exchange

Most Bitcoin exchanges will also allow you to buy Bitcoin Cash, here are the top ones around.

Buy Bitcoin Cash Through eToro.

eToro allows users from around the world to buy and sell Bitcoin Cash with a variety of payment methods.

eToro doesn't give you actual access to your coins, and you can't send coins from eToro to other people. The only thing that can be done with the platform is to buy and sell Bitcoin Cash for fiat currency (i.e., Dollars, Euros, etc.).

If you use eToro, you don't need a Bitcoin Cash wallet as they don't supply you the actual coins.

Bitcoin can widely fluctuate in prices and are not appropriate for all investors. Any EU regulatory framework does not supervise trading Bitcoin. So keep in mind that your capital is at risk.

Buy Bitcoin Cash Through Coinmama

Coinmama one of the oldest exchanges around, allows you to buy Bitcoin Cash with a credit card, debit card or SEPA transfer. Coinmama accepts users from almost all countries around the world.

Buy Bitcoin Cash Through CEX.io

CEX.io, based in London, is a trusted, old name in the industry, having been around since 2013. You can choose from a selection of cryptocurrencies on the site, including Bitcoin Cash.

The exchange has a brokerage service (easier to use, more expensive) and a trading platform (cheaper but more complicated).CEX accepts credit cards, debit cards, wire transfers, and SEPA.

Coinbase - The most reputable Bitcoin exchange around, Coinbase supplies Bitcoin Cash support and buy/sell options. Coinbase allows you to get competitive rates if you live in one of the 33 supported countries around the world.

Buy Bitcoin Cash Through Coinbase

Coinbase is a reputable Bitcoin exchange that supplies a variety of other services including a wallet, a trading platform (Coinbase Pro) and a Bitcoin debit card.

If you're a beginner, it's probably best to use the brokerage service, which is a bit more expensive, but more comfortable to use. Advanced users can use Coinbase Pro to buy Bitcoin Cash with lower fees.

Buy Bitcoin Cash Through Bitstamp

Bitstamp the oldest exchange around supports the trading of BCH to Bitcoin and direct purchases with US dollars or Euros. There's also an option to buy Bitcoin Cash with your credit card at a higher price.

If you know your way around Bitcoin trading platforms, it's best to use that service and not the credit card service since you'll save substantially on fees.

Other options to purchase Bitcoin Cash include Bitfinex, Kraken, Poloniex, HitBTC, and more (you can view all available exchange on Bitcoin Cash's website).

Differences Between Bitcoin Cash and Bitcoin

Did you know that Bitcoin Cash originated from Bitcoin itself? That's right — Bitcoin Cash nodes were once a part of the Bitcoin blockchain. Bitcoin Cash is a fork of Bitcoin.

But which of the two should you choose to invest in? What is the difference between Bitcoin Cash vs. Bitcoin? What's a "fork'? There are so many questions.

By the end of this guide, you will know the difference between two different cryptocurrencies – Bitcoin Cash vs. Bitcoin. You will learn more about their history, value, and potential for the future.

First, let's look closer at Bitcoin and its background.

Bitcoin

Bitcoin was the first-ever cryptocurrency, and for many years it wasn't very well known. It is just like any other real currency. You can use it to buy, sell and trade for goods, services, investments and more.

The blockchain technology that it's made of prevents it from being counterfeited. It also means it is not owned, issued, or controlled by anyone single group or party.

For example, the US dollar is issued by the US government and is controlled by banks. In this scenario, the central parties are the government and the banks. When you transfer dollars to a friend, you are relying on the bank to authorize and process the transaction.

Bitcoin, on the other hand, is not issued or controlled by any central authority. The computers that run the blockchain verifies the transactions on the blockchain, and anybody can own these computers — the blockchain is decentralized.

On the blockchain, transactions are stored and submitted in blocks. The computers verify the entire block of transactions at once by solving a complicated math problem. When the problem is solved, the transactions in the block are tested, and new Bitcoin is created — it is given to the computer that solved the problem. This process is called mining!

As more people try to get their hands on some Bitcoin, and the rate of creation decreases, the common belief is that the value will increase. That is why so many people are crazy about Bitcoin now!

Today, Bitcoin is the most valuable cryptocurrency currently on the market. While other currencies are attempting to outrank Bitcoin and reduce its dominance over the digital-coin sector, few are getting close. However, Bitcoin Cash may be an exception to that due to the difference between Bitcoin and Bitcoin Cash!

A Fork

There are quite a few Bitcoin forks, but none are as used or as well known as Bitcoin Cash. A fork is created when the original code of a blockchain is updated, but only some of the nodes (computers) on the blockchain accept the update.

The original blockchain (like Bitcoin) remains the same, and the updated nodes split off from the original blockchain and create a new blockchain (like Bitcoin Cash) and the coins on the blockchain become separate and unique from the ones on the original blockchain.

Anyone holding the original coin at the time it was forked will automatically get the forked version of the coin they were holding. So, when Bitcoin forked to Bitcoin Cash, someone who had 10 BTC would automatically have received a certain number of BCH matching the value of their 10 BTC.

Now then, let's talk about Bitcoin Cash itself.

Bitcoin Cash

Like Bitcoin, Bitcoin Cash is a cryptocurrency with its blockchain. It works just like a digital currency, and new BCH (Bitcoin Cash) is created through Bitcoin Cash mining. It was built at the end of 2016, making it much younger than Bitcoin.

Bitcoin was forked to create Bitcoin Cash because the developers of Bitcoin wanted to make some important changes to Bitcoin. The developers of the Bitcoin community could not agree with some of the changes that they wanted to make. So, a small group of these developers forked Bitcoin to create a new version of the same code with a few modifications.

The changes that make all the difference between Bitcoin Cash vs. Bitcoin are these:

- Bitcoin Cash has cheaper transfer fees (around $0.20 per transaction), so making transactions in BCH will save you more money than using BTC. A BTC transaction can cost around USD 1 per transaction, although it previously went up to around $25 per transaction.

- BCH has faster transfer times. So, you don't have to wait the 10 minutes it takes to verify a Bitcoin transaction.

- BCH can handle more transactions per second. This means that more people can use BCH at the same time than they can with BTC.

- All these changes are because a Bitcoin Cash block (in the blockchain) is eight times bigger than a Bitcoin block. This makes BCH faster, cheaper, and more scalable than Bitcoin. Bitcoin cash is becoming more and more adopted by the day because of this.

Bitcoin Cash vs. Bitcoin: The Price War

As mentioned earlier, cryptocurrencies like Bitcoin or Bitcoin Cash derive their value from how much they are adopted, used, and demanded. We can analyze them in terms of ROI (return on investment) and value growth.

They are both holders of value, and while Bitcoin has been the holder of the most value up until now, Bitcoin Cash is gaining users and value fast.

Bitcoin Cash is still quite young. So, it is still in the stage of capturing and realizing its place in the crypto market. Many people speculate that Bitcoin Cash might take a good portion of Bitcoin's market share, making it the new dominant crypto in the industry. This is because Bitcoin Cash has addressed the scaling issues that Bitcoin faces, allowing more people to use it with ease and lower fees.

If the Bitcoin developer community doesn't find a way to agree to a mutual update to the Bitcoin code to fix its problems, Bitcoin might lose in the war between BTC vs. BCH. This means that more people will likely switch to using BCH as their main store of value and transactional currency.

In the recent past, Bitcoin Cash has been worth as low as 5% of Bitcoin, to as high as 33%. It is currently staying within the range of 10-15% of the price of Bitcoin.

One of the things holding BCH's rapid growth back is the confusion people have between Bitcoin and Bitcoin Cash. Many newbie investors see Bitcoin Cash as a cheaper Bitcoin with a lower entry point to the market. This is because they share very similar names and come from the same branding and community.

The confusion has also led to Bitcoin Cash receiving negative attention as a copycat currency that is simply a cash grab, aimed at tricking new crypto investors into buying a fake Bitcoin. This, however, is not true.

BCH is no fake Bitcoin, but it may very well be a better one.

Bitcoin Cash vs. Bitcoin: The Features

Bitcoin Cash Advantages

The main advantage of Bitcoin Cash is that it is cheaper and faster to use. This is because it is more scalable, meaning that more people can transact on the blockchain at any given time.

Its development team is quick to implement solutions that make the blockchain more scalable, which gives it great future potential for adoption and use.

It is also cheaper to move around between exchanges. Whenever its price surges, it is a great trading asset against Bitcoin and a solid investment to hedge against Bitcoin, should Bitcoin lose its market dominance one day.

Note: Nothing in this article is financial advice. You should always consult a financial advisor before investing.

Bitcoin Cash Disadvantages

Bitcoin Cash does not have as much investor confidence as Bitcoin. Also, its adoption rate and market penetration is much lower than Bitcoin's. This has a lot to do with the fact that this coin is much newer than Bitcoin.

While the price of BCH is around 10-15% of the price of Bitcoin, the cost of Bitcoin Cash mining is relatively the same as mining Bitcoin. This means that someone who mines Bitcoin Cash makes 50-60% less profit than someone mining Bitcoin with the same e🔲uipment. For this reason, miners are not as 🔲uick to mine Bitcoin Cash.

Finally, when it comes to trading, BCH has far less trading pairs than BTC, making it less tradeable than Bitcoin. All these disadvantages work towards making Bitcoin Cash's adoption rates and prices much lower than Bitcoin's.

Bitcoin Advantages Over Bitcoin Cash

As the original cryptocurrency, Bitcoin is the base currency of the entire sector. It is what all other cryptocurrencies trade against (as well as ETH, most of the time) and is tradable on most exchanges. Bitcoin is the most popular and has the most trading pairs with other cryptocurrencies.

As of 23rd March 2018, Bitcoin makes up 44.5% of the entire capital of the crypto-sector and is considered the Gold standard of a rapidly growing industry.

The biggest advantage Bitcoin has over Bitcoin Cash is its community and the cult-like following: it's the first cryptocurrency anyone hears about.

Bitcoin Disadvantages Over Bitcoin Cash

The disadvantages of Bitcoin when compared to Bitcoin Cash mainly regard the scalability issues facing Bitcoin. Bitcoin is older, slower, and costs a lot more per transaction. It is likely that as the sector grows, Bitcoin will continue to lose its dominance to these other coins.

Another disadvantage is that the core development team of Bitcoin is not united as good as other crypto teams, like that of Ether, for example. They appear to be divided as a group and lacking clear leadership.

This implements scaling solutions which are more challenging to agree on and implement to the network — not good at all.

Bitcoin Cash vs. Bitcoin: Where Can You Buy Them?

One of the most popular exchanges to buy both Bitcoin and Bitcoin Cash is Coinbase.

On this platform, you can use fiat to buy popular cryptocurrencies (including Bitcoin and Bitcoin Cash) through your credit card, bank account, and more. Unfortunately, Coinbase is only currently available in 32 countries:

U.S.A., Canada, UK, Switzerland, Sweden, Spain, Slovenia, San Marino, Portugal, Poland, Norway, Netherlands, Monaco, Malta, Liechtenstein, Latvia, Jersey, Italy, Ireland, Hungary, Greece, Finland, Denmark, Czech Republic, Cyprus, Croatia, Bulgaria, Belgium, Austria, Australia and Singapore.

If you are not in one of these countries and you want to buy Bitcoin Cash or Bitcoin, you can try out other broker exchanges like CoinMama or CEX.io.

If you use a broker that doesn't sell BCH but sells BTC, you can always buy Bitcoin and exchange it for Bitcoin Cash on a trading platform like Binance.

Another option for buying these coins with cash is to do so on a P2P exchange, like LocalBitcoins. Again, you'll only be able to buy Bitcoin on P2P exchanges, but you can trade your BTC for BCH using a trading exchange afterward.

Bitcoin Cash vs. Bitcoin: Conclusion

Many people are under the impression that Bitcoin Cash vs. Bitcoin is a war, and that one should be better than the other. For practical reasons,

Bitcoin Cash is a faster and cheaper asset to use for transacting on the blockchain.

But Bitcoin, being the original cryptocurrency, is the most adopted and currently the greatest store of value in the cryptomarket. This leads me to believe that both these coins can remain as staples in the industry as it evolves and matures.

BCH can become the main tool for transactions and moving money around as more users adopt it. BTC can continue to be used as a store of value that is considered the gold of digital currency. Both stand to grow in value and adoption over time, making them worthy investments for any investor to look into and consider.

Now that you know the differences between these two coins, you can better decide how you want to invest in them and how you will use them.

For example, you can invest in Bitcoin Cash to use it as your main form of currency to transact with. However, you could invest in Bitcoin the way you would invest in gold – for investment benefits.

Types of Bitcoin & Crypto Wallets

One needs to look for the following things when selecting a reliable Bitcoin wallet, irrespective of whether it is a software or **a hardware wallet:**

- **Control private keys** – A wallet where you own and control your keys.
- **Backup & security features** – Seed backup keys and pin codes.
- **Developer community** – Active development community for maintenance.
- **Ease of use** – Elegant UI for fast and easy use.
- **Compatibility** – Compatible on different operating systems.

Now that you know what to look for in a Bitcoin wallet let's check out the types of Bitcoin wallets.

- **Ledger Nano X**

Ledger Nano X is a hardware wallet from a French start-up. This is a modern and functional Bitcoin wallet.This hardware wallet works with desktop and mobile and comes with in-built battery.

From the security perspective, it has two chips (1 is for secure element) which ensure your private keys never get exposed to the world.

You can store up to 100+ cryptocurrencies and using Ledger Nano X; you can use it as a login for many exchanges.

Some of the supported coins by **Ledger Nano X are:**

- ✓ Bitcoin
- ✓ Ethereum
- ✓ Litecoin
- ✓ Ripple (XRP)
- ✓ Binance chain (BNB)
- ✓ Dash
- ✓ Cardona (ADA)
- ✓ EOS (EOS)
- ✓ USDT
- ✓ Tron
- ✓ Monero (XMR)
- ✓ All ERC 20 Token
- ✓ USDC
- ✓ BAT (Basic attention token)

- **Ledger Nano S**

This the early version of Ledger Nano X and It's like a USB drive which connects to any USB port. It doesn't have a battery and only starts up when plugged into a computer (or mobile device).

The Ledger doesn't come with an anti-tampering sticker as its cryptographic procedure checks for the integrity of the instrument when powered on.

It also comes with an OLED screen and two side buttons for confirming transactions.

When you configure your Nano S as a new device, you need to set up your pin code to secure your wallet. After that, note down and store your 24-word recovery phrase. This recovery phrase can be used anytime to restore your bitcoins.

With this wallet, your private keys are stored offline, so you need not worry about the safety of your coins.

Nano S is also the cheapest multi-currency hardware wallet (approx $120).

The Ledger Nano S wallet supports the following **major cryptocurrencies:**

- ✓ Bitcoin (BTC)
- ✓ Bitcoin Cash (BCC)
- ✓ Ethereum (ETH)
- ✓ Ethereum Classic (ETC)
- ✓ Litecoin (LTC)
- ✓ Dash (DASH)
- ✓ Dogecoin (DOGE)
- ✓ Zcash (ZEC)
- ✓ Ripple (XRP)
- ✓ Stratis (STRAT)
- ✓ Komodo (KMD)
- ✓ PoSW

- ✓ ARK
- ✓ Ubi🔲
- ✓ Expanse (EXP)
- ✓ PIVX
- ✓ Vertcoin
- ✓ Viacoin
- ✓ Stealthcoin (XST)
- ✓ NEO (Works with NEON Wallet and supports GAS too)
- ✓ Bitcoin Gold & more...

Also, it is a multi-currency wallet where you can store/manage more than 700 coins and ERC20 tokens all at once place.

Note: You should always use a hardware wallet when you have a lot of bitcoins or altcoins.

- **Trezor**

Presented by SatoshiLabs, a Czech Republic-based company, Trezor is the world's first Bitcoin hardware wallet.

It is a small device with an OLED screen, which connects via a USB to your personal computer or phone. Its fundamental purpose is to store your private keys offline and sign transactions.

The initial setup is a bit different from the Ledger Nano S.

With Trezor, when you first connect it to your PC, it shows a nine-digit pin code on its OLED screen. You need to enter the same pin code by clicking on your corresponding PC screen. This code is generated randomly every time you connect Trezor and makes sure that even a tampered PC can't get your pin.

After entering the pin, you will be asked to write your 24-word recovery seed. Again, you need to keep your recovery key safe because this is the only way you will be able to restore your bitcoins.

Trezor now supports **many cryptocurrencies:**

- ✓ BTC – Bitcoin
- ✓ ETH/ETC – Ethereum/Ethereum Classic
- ✓ NMC – Namecoin
- ✓ LTC – Litecoin
- ✓ DOGE – Dogecoin
- ✓ ZEC – Zcash
- ✓ DASH – Dash

Trezor can be used with apps such as TREZOR Wallet, Mycelium, and Multibit HD.

It is available now for Windows (version 7 and higher), OS X (version 10.8 and higher), and Linux. You can also use it with your Android devices.

Bitcoin Wallets Based on Connectivity

Hot Bitcoin Wallets (Online)

Wallets in which bitcoins are stored online and which are connected 24/7 to the internet are called hot wallets. Such Bitcoin platforms and services which can receive/withdraw bitcoins for their users are hot wallets. They are very much like the wallet you have in your pocket.

Akin to a cashier in a bank who has not kept the money deposited in the bank vault but left it on his/her desk, your bitcoins are always under threat when placed online and connected 24/7.

Why are hot wallets good?

- The easiest way to store small amounts of bitcoin and crypto
- practice issuing and receiving payments are quick and easy
- Some active portfolios provide access to funds on multiple devices.

Why are hot wallets bad?

- It is not safe to store large amounts of bitcoins and encrypted files securely.

Cold Bitcoin Wallets (Offline)

And you must have guessed, those bitcoins stored offline in hard drives or USB drives or paper, away from internet connectivity are called cold wallets.

Why are hardware wallets good?

- The easiest way to securely store bitcoins and other currencies.
- Accessible to backup and secure
- less margin of error; configuration is easy even for less technical users

Why are hardware wallets bad?

- They are not free.

Bitcoin Wallets Based on Custodianship of Keys

Custodial Wallets (3rd Party Services)

When you entrust your bitcoins to be held by some agency/exchange on your behalf, it means you are trusting them and storing your bitcoins with them on their servers, thereby giving them custody of your bitcoins.

Non-Custodial Wallets

When you entrust your bitcoins to nobody and take responsibility for your funds by saving your Bitcoin private keys yourself, such wallets are called non-custodial wallets.

Which Bitcoin Wallet Should You Use?

It is a tricky question. The type of wallet you should use depends on your level of activity and level of security with which you want to handle your bitcoins.

It also depends on how frequently you use your funds and how much you want to store on any particular wallet. Also, are the bitcoins you possess for your savings/investment, or are they for daily transactions?

You can use hardware wallets like Ledger Nano X for storing a significant amount of bitcoins because of the high-security features. You can also use desktop wallets to keep bitcoins, which you might be not used for daily transactions. So that whenever required, you can quickly connect your desktop wallet to the Bitcoin network and transfer bitcoins.

Web wallets or mobile wallet to keep small amounts of bitcoins, similar to a wallet in your pocket for daily transactions.

Hardware Wallets: Keep Your Coins Safe

Hardware wallets aren't free. But the price can be worth it if you own a significant amount of coins. A hardware wallet will protect a few hundred in Bitcoin/ crypto just as effectively as a few million. Hardware wallet keeps private keys separate from vulnerable, interconnected devices. Your all-important keys are maintained in a secure offline environment on the hardware wallet, fully protected even should the device be plugged into a malware-infected computer. Generating and storing private keys offline using a hardware wallet ensures that hackers have no way to reach your coins.

Hackers would have to steal the hardware wallet itself, but even then, it can be protected with a pin code. Don't worry about your hardware wallet getting stolen, lost or damaged either; so long as you create a secret backup code, you can always retrieve your coins.

How Hardware Wallets Work

A hardware wallet is a physical, electronic device that is designed to protect an individual's cryptocurrency funds by securing their private keys. The idea behind hardware wallets is to isolate the private keys from online methods of storage, such as a computer or smartphone, which are more susceptible to being compromised by a hacker. Storing your private keys offline prevents against this, as hackers would have to physically steal your hardware wallet to gain access to a user's private keys. But even then, most hardware wallets re?uire a PIN code for access, providing an added layer of protection.

Are Display Screens Important For a Hardware Wallet?

Using a touch screen with a great UI is easy and intuitive to everyone, and it is what makes ELLIPAL uni?ue. However, do you know that it is also a significant security boost?

Screens are just not for displays. **Here are how a nice clear and large screen can improve your security:**

- Confirm addresses
- Confirm transactions
- Confirm Mnemonics

In addition to the large display screen helps you to keep your coins in check. The display screen cannot be hacked, so do not worry if it will ever show false information.

Best Bitcoin Hardware Wallet

- **Ledger Nano X**

The Ledger Nano X is Ledger's newest hardware wallet. The main idea behind the device is that it is the easiest way to secure your Bitcoin and other Cryptocurrencies as well. The main benefit is that it has Bluetooth, making it the first hardware wallet that connects with IOS devices. Its more secure than using just an app on your phone, because all transactions are signed with the NANO X. The Ledger Nano X supports an extensive list of cryptocurrencies, including popular assets like Bitcoin, Ethereum, XRP, Litecoin and more. Ledger is continuously expanding its crypto-asset coverage with both apps developed by Ledger and apps developed by the community and extensively tested by Ledger.

- **Ledger Nano S**

The Nano S has a sleek design, intuitive user interface, and wide support of altcoins. While many hardware wallets on the market feature a "simple" chip, all Ledger hardware wallets are equipped with a "smart card chip," that includes a secure element. This kind of chip is used for highly secure applications, such as protecting biometric data on passports or credit card information. Secure element chips are complicated and costly to hack, while "simple" chips, even with software protection, require much less effort. The Ledger Nano S can simultaneously run up to 18 device applications. Even if you uninstall a device application, the private keys to access your crypto assets remain secure. You'll always be able to manage your assets by simply re-installing the application on your Ledger device.

- **Trezor one**

Trezor launched in August 2014 as the first Bitcoin hardware wallet, offering secure Bitcoin storage plus the ability to spend with the convenience of a hot wallet. Trezor is a small, thumb-sized device which connects to your computer with a USB cable. It stores your Bitcoin and cryptocurrency private keys offline and signs transactions. It can be safely used on a malware-infected computer. Trezor provides top-notch security for bitcoin, protecting against both physical and virtual theft. Trezor is an HD wallet where you control the private keys so that an entire wallet can be backed up with the 24 words generated on setup. A pin code is required on setup and required for spending. TREZOR and the Ledger Nano S are often compared. The main difference is that TREZOR is more like a mini-computer, while the Ledger Nano S uses a secure chip.

- **KeepKey**

KeepKey was released in September 2015 and was the second hardware Bitcoin wallet to offer a screen. The KeepKey's larger screen gives it some extra security features that the Nano S and Trezor lack. The high price tag is due to its digital screen, metal body, and high level of security. KeepKey's pin code and number randomization make sure that 1) your wallet is secure from physical theft and 2) that a hacker couldn't steal bitcoins from your wallet with malware. KeepKey is an HD wallet, meaning your entire wallet can be backed up with the 12 words generated on setup. Twelve words is the default setting, although KeepKey supports seed lengths of 18 and 24.

Hot Wallets

Hot wallets are called hot because they are connected to the Internet, which generally means it's easier for hackers to hack into and steal your valuable coins from you. Examples of hot wallets include those free wallets at your favorite bitcoin exchange website like Coinbase or Kraken and mobile app wallets.

Desktop Wallet

Desktop wallets are another form of hot wallets, especially if you install it on a system that's connected to the Internet. However, you do have control over your private keys, and you can encrypt your wallet to prevent hacking attempts. The only downside to desktop wallets is if your computer gets destroyed or stolen, then you can pretty much say goodbye to your bitcoins.

There have been many instances of theft in hot wallets. Some hackers have even managed to steal millions of dollars' worth of bitcoins! Hot wallets are great for storing small amounts and transacting on the fly.

Online Bitcoin Wallets (Web Wallets)

Third parties manage web wallets in general – that is they hold the private keys and the public keys of the user – meaning that the process of accessing Bitcoin or any cryptocurrency is significantly lowered – you don't have to download the full client or acquaint yourself with various forms and methods inherent in wallet software.

The trade-off though is that the third party is responsible for maintaining the integrity of your wallet and keeping the private keys secret – you need to trust them as they could just run off with the money – and there is no Government based insurance scheme to guarantee deposits.

The advantages of web wallets – apart from the general simplicity – is the ability to bundle transactions together before pushing them onto the blockchain and therefore lowering transaction fees. They can also perform internal transfers for zero fees as an attraction to pull in customers and increase their user base – a bitcoin ecosystem within the bitcoin ecosystem – again coinbase is the perfect example of this, whilst offering wallet, exchange and Point of Sale services – they have garnered a very large market share pushing other payment services such as Bitpay to adopt the same strategy and vertically integrate into wallet services from Point of Sales and exchange provision.

GreenAddress

GreenAddress is a bitcoin wallet with a web interface that is also available for desktop, iOS, and Android. They use 2-of-2 signatures, one which the user holds, the other from GreenAddress.

They have a watch-only login mode that keeps you and your wallet private and secure while still enabling you to check your balances and transactions, but without giving potential threats (e.g., if you're on public wifi) access to your funds or wallet settings. GreenAddress also has a ⊠uick PIN login for your devices.

Android Bitcoin Wallets

Bitcoin Android wallets are apps that allow you to store, send, and receive your Bitcoin from your Android device. While using a mobile wallet will enable you to make payments quickly and easily, mobile wallets are always connected to the Internet (i.e., hot wallets), and this makes them more vulnerable to attacks. Moreover, mobile devices tend to get lost, broken, or stolen ⊠uite often, so extra steps are re⊠uired to secure your coins when using a mobile Android wallet.

Here are the best Bitcoin wallets for Android:

- **MyCelium**

MyCelium is a popular mobile app wallet that features a wealth of advanced privacy and security features. Yes, the wallet can be a bit complicated for newbie users, but it's still one of the safest and fastest on the market. As an open-source software program, MyCelium is constantly being upgraded. The wallet doesn't have a web or desktop interface, meaning coins can be accessed only through your mobile wallet.

- **Coinomi**

Coinomi is a secure, cryptocurrency wallet that offers exchange capabilities within the app. Coinomi considers itself to be security and privacy-focused emphasizing the fact that no identity linking is possible from within the wallet. Thanks to its speedy installation and setup and multiple coin support, the wallet is trendy among crypto enthusiasts as a way to store and exchange cryptocurrency.

- **Edge**

Edge, previously known as Airbitz, is a multi-currency, open-source mobile Bitcoin wallet. Thanks to the open-source development of the product, Edge is considered to be exceptionally secure. On top of that, Edge also offers beginner-friendly features, such as a list of businesses that accept bitcoin. Edge's partnerships with Bitcoin-accepting business often provide discounts for users who make purchases via the app. The wallet is also available in an iOS version.

- **BRD (formerly BreadWallet)**

BRD is probably one of the most straightforward Bitcoin Android wallets around. The wallet is open source, which makes it more secure and reliable. No registration is required to use the app. Once the app is installed, you can instantly start sending or receiving Bitcoin. The app also offers an exchange on which you can buy your assets and store them directly on your wallet. On the downside, the app only allows a basic set of features and therefore is more suitable for beginners and not advanced users.

- **Abra**

Abra is a mobile Bitcoin wallet which also allows you to trade and exchange cryptocurrency for fiat. As a wallet, Abra will enable you to store not only Bitcoin but also Bitcoin Cash and Litecoin on the wallet. An additional 27 coins can be traded through the app but not stored on it. Using the wallet requires you to provide your email address and phone number. For users who wish to stay anonymous, this is a significant drawback. However, the apps interface and overall experience is delightful and easy to use, even for a complete newbie.

iOS and iPhone Bitcoin Wallets

Bitcoin iOS wallets are apps that allow you to store, send & receive your Bitcoin from your iPhone or iPad. This type of wallet gives you the convenience of making payments quickly and easily from anywhere, as long as you have your mobile device with you. However, this convenience comes with a price. Not only this is a hot wallet (i.e., a wallet the is connected to the Internet) which by design is less secure, it is also stored on a mobile device which can be easily stolen, broken or just get lost.

- **Bread**

Also known as Breadwallet (previously), this is unanimously the market-leading mobile-wallet preferred for iOS. It is a real standalone bitcoin client; in fact, the first iOS wallet to be so. It has no server that could be hacked, or that could go down. Also, as it is directly connected to the Bitcoin network using SPV mode, it does not charge anything extra for transactions. This is an extremely lightweight app and thus sits easily on the phone.

- **Edge**

Edge is an open-source, multi-currency mobile Bitcoin wallet. In addition to its excellent security score, Edge is also known for its beginner-friendly features, such as listings of merchants that accept bitcoin, and ways to buy discounted gift cards. Edge is also known to have partnerships with Bitcoin-accepting business, which often provide some discount when using the app to make purchases.

- **DropBit**

With DropBit, all you need is the contact list, already in your phone, and you can send someone their first amount of Bitcoin. You don't need the recipient to have a Bitcoin address or have their wallet already established.

- **Desktop wallets**

Desktop wallets are programs that store and manage the private key for your Bitcoins on your computer's hard drive.

- **Electrum**

- ✓ Electrum is one of the oldest and time-tested Bitcoin wallet developed by a voluntary developer in November 2011.
- ✓ It is an open-source project released under an MIT license.
- ✓ Moreover, it is a lightweight wallet, meaning you need not download the whole blockchain for sync.

Also, it is a self-hosted wallet, which means by using Electrum, you are your bank where you control your seed and PIN.

This lightweight desktop bitcoin wallet supports multiple operating systems such as Windows, Mac, etc. It is integrated with premium hardware wallets such as TREZOR, KeepKey and Ledger Nano S.

Bitcoin Banks: $1 Billion Lost In Hacks

One last thing to keep in mind when it comes to Bitcoin wallet, there is a difference between a wallet and a wallet bank. Some Bitcoin users consider Coinbase a Bitcoin wallet, but these companies operate much more like banks.

Do not forget:

Private keys must protect users from being able to use the Bitcoin network safely without being stolen. When you give someone else control over your private keys, you essentially deposit in that financial institution, just like a deposit in a bank.

Do not keep coins on the stock market. Bitcoin users have lost more than $ 1 billion in bitcoins in exchange for hacking and scams. Use your private keys.

This does not mean that bitcoin banks are inherently bad. Companies such as Coinbase have done wonders to attract more users into the ecosystem. It is important to remember that the person who manages the private keys manages the bitcoins associated with these keys.

A misunderstanding on this point has already generated hundreds of millions of dollars. It is therefore essential to understand this essential difference between how Bitcoin private keys can be stored.

Understanding the operation of bitcoin wallet is an important aspect of the security of using this new technology. Bitcoin is still in the early years of development, and portfolios will be much easier to use in time.

Soon, some devices may come with pre-installed wallets that communicate with the blockchain without the user's knowledge.

For the moment, it is essential to keep in mind that private keys are what you need to protect if you want to protect your bitcoin against hackers, user errors, and other potential problems.

Theft And Scams

Whatever wallet you choose, always **remember:**

Your bitcoins are only secure if the private key is securely generated, it remains a secret and, more importantly, you only manage it!

Here are two examples where users have been ripped off by leaving bitcoins to a third party:

- The tip of Bitfinex, where users lost 70 million dollars
- Mt Gox failed, where users lost $ 450 million or more

Follow these three basic principles to prevent theft, scams, **and other loss of resources:**

1. Generate your private keys in a secure and offline environment. (Except when trivial amounts are used, in which case the keys can be created in an active portfolio).

2. Save your private keys. This helps protect you from losing your bitcoins due to a failed hard drive or other problem or accident. Ideally, you need a dual set of off-site backups to protect you from fire, theft, and more.

3. Encrypt portfolios to provide additional security. This helps prevent physical theft of your money if your device or hardware portfolio is stolen.

Securing your bitcoins properly is an essential step for every Bitcoin user.

With Bitcoin, you have the privilege, but also the responsibility, to protect your own money. There have been countless Bitcoin scams that could have been avoided if people had not trusted their bitcoins to others. It's a good rule never to trust anyone with your money.

Bitcoin Wallets: Frequently Asked Questions

Bitcoin Wallets. What Are They?

With Bitcoin wallets, we can send, receive, and store quantities of Bitcoins in the Satoshi unit. Wallets protect funds by protecting our private keys. These private keys are proof of ownership of our Bitcoins. As such, a Bitcoin wallet is key to your safe blockchain.

What is a Private Key?

Private keys have emerged as a means of communicating securely via unsecured communication channels.

Historically, the biggest weakness of cryptography before the advent of public-key cryptography has been the inability to communicate the "key" that gives meaning to encrypted messages. The solution was to use two keys (public and private).

It's a little trick. The keys come in pairs. The public key is used to encrypt the message, while the private key decrypts it. You are the only person with the private key. Everyone is free to have their public key. As a result, everyone can send you encrypted messages without having to agree on a password. Just use your public key, and you'll unravel the babble language with your private key.

Why Should I Care About Private Keys?

In the end, all of this can be neglected without much danger. Remember, it's good to know what you're dealing with. Bitcoin wallets use a fundamental cryptographic principle that we use for things ranging from https to websites or sending anonymous suggestions to Wikileaks. More importantly, by understanding the private keys, it will be much easier to get ac?uainted with the cold storage wallets.

What is a Bitcoin Address

A Bitcoin address is like an account number, but better. The address indicates which wallet the coins should be sent to. Like a bank account number, the difference lies in multi-address wallets. These can be adjusted, including payment re?uest information, such as an amount and an expiration date.

What should I know about addresses?

Bitcoin wallet addresses are case-sensitive, typically contain 34 characters and lowercase letters, begin with 1 or 3, and never use 0, 0, 1, and I to make each address character as clear as possible. It's a lot to assimilate. But do not worry. What they consist of is largely irrelevant for you. You only need to know that it is a string that indicates a destination in the Bitcoin Blockchain.

How do I generate a bitcoin address for my wallet?

How to generate a new Bitcoin address differs depending on the wallet. Some manage their addresses for you. Others give you total control. As with many other Bitcoin technologies, the option to get your hands dirty is always open.

If you take the simplest way, press a button to generate a new address for your wallet. With some wallets, such as Electrum, you can choose how many blocks your transaction should confirm. The more you want your payment to be made ?uickly, the more you will have to pay the miners to verify your activity. Here we find another difference between Bitcoin wallets and bank accounts. With the right wallet, the control and monitoring of our transactions are much more extensive than those of the traditional banking system.

How do I fund a Bitcoin Wallet?

Start by buying Bitcoins. Make an exchange in your country, ask a friend to share if you want a more fluid experience. Purchased coins can be sent to your wallet by specifying one of their addresses.

With some wallets, especially online, you can also buy coins. Keep in mind that these have greater margins of change than it is better to leave them alone.

Is Bitcoin Safe?

Is Bitcoin a safe way to digitally store value? Are we wise to store our coins on our computer? Indeed, online wallets are inherently more dangerous than offline wallets. Even offline wallets can be violated, which means that security in the Bitcoin world largely depends on good practice. Just as you would avoid shaking your accounts in a dangerous place, you need to make sure your passwords and passwords are as secure as possible.

How do I open a bitcoin account?

For some people, this may seem like a strange question. The truth is that people from a financial or commercial background probably expect Bitcoin to be a direct alternative to our current financial system. This is not the case.

You do not need a Bitcoin account. There is not such a thing. You only need a wallet. The only accounts you can find are separate online wallets in different accounts via a user system.

How do I know which is best for me?

It is not reasonable to expect someone else to make that decision for you. After all, your preference depends entirely on your personality and your needs. So be honest with yourself.

You should not need anything complicated if you use the wallet for simple Internet-related problems or to save money. However, if you plan to run a Bitcoin business, you must use advanced wallets that support automated mass payments.

Any potential mistakes to be aware of?

First of all, do not throw your money into a foreign exchange wallet. Store your coins in an environment where you have total control.

Secondly, do not keep all your coins in one place. You will be crushed if you lose access to a wallet with all your money.

Third, check the destination address. Transactions in bitcoins can not be canceled, so never lose your coins for the benefit of a stranger.

Finally, use reliable online portfolios (if you have one). Do not trust anyone with your money. Make sure the online wallet provider is reputed to meet the highest possible security standards.

What other types of wallets can I use?

Other types of wallets are hot wallets. This means that wallets run on a computer connected to the Internet.

Android, iOS, and desktop wallets are all examples of this.

How many backups of my seed should I create?

It is recommended that you keep at least two backup copies of your seeds at different locations.

You can also laminate your seeds to protect them from water or other damage. If you store your seeds in fireproof safes, you can protect them in the event of a burn at the storage location.

Another option is to place your seeds in metal using stamps or Billfodl manually.

What happened if someone finds my 24-word seeds?

Unless you use a word of 25 if someone finds your seed of 24 words, he/she can erase your entire wallet.

Coinbase

Coinbase is a web portfolio with a simple design and a series of useful features that make it an excellent choice for beginners. You can send and receive bitcoins via email, and you can buy and sell bitcoins directly from Coinbase.

Once you have mastered everything, it's best to move your Coinbase coins to the wallet mentioned above because Ledger Nano S. Coinbase is a good place to buy bitcoins and learn how it works, but it's not a good long-term storage solution.

A full Android app gives you access to all features of the account along the way. The founders of Coinbase have proven themselves and raised funds from huge venture capitalists. This gives Coinbase an unparalleled level of legitimacy in the Bitcoin space. They are also one of the few big Bitcoin companies to never suffer from major hacking.

Electrum

Electrum is a software wallet with which you can quickly configure a high level of security. During the simple installation process, you get a 12-word phrase that you can use to restore all your bitcoins in the event of a computer crash. Your wallet is also encrypted as standard, protecting your currencies against hackers. Electrum is available for Windows, OSX, and Linux and is the recommended software wallet for beginners.

Other Wallets

It is also recommended some other wallets, but not for the novice Bitcoin user. If you are ready for a major challenge, Armory is a good option for those who need the greatest security possible. The original Bitcoin-Qt client is also reliable and deserves to be taught how to use it.

DigitalBitbox

The DigitalBitbox seems to be the product of paranoid fever dreams of a too clear mind. Most genuine cryptocurrency enthusiasts tend to be wrong about security.

By way of comparison: DigitalBitbox's manufacturers live there permanently. This is by no means a bad thing because Shift devices may have created the safest storage device for crypto-currencies outside of paper storage.

The DigitalBitbox is not only a very well protected device, but it also offers several other features that help it to expand and distinguish itself from the competition.

The First Rule of DigitalBitbox is Security

Just like most crypto-assets devices for cold storage, DigitalBitbox looks like a standard USB drive. The only thing that distinguishes it from hardware wallets is the micro SD card that is integrated horizontally in the middle. This function distinguishes it not only visually but also functionally.

The most important selling point of this hardware wallet is that it is no longer necessary to write several secret phrases to recover your assets in an emergency. When you set up DigitalBitbox for the first time, all this information is automatically saved to the SD card. This can save investors a lot of headaches in the future. OK, you must always make sure that the SD card is kept in a safe place and that you only need it in the DigitalBitbox during setup or when restarting.

The Second Rule of DigitalBitbox is also Security.

In addition to this outstanding security feature, this new hardware portfolio includes several other features that enhance your overall security or extend its use to more than just storing your Bitcoins. The most important of these features is the ability to create a "hidden" secondary wallet: marketed by the manufacturer as "plausible refusal." The most important idea here is that you have to store most of your resources in a less accessible portfolio and the rest in the more visible. If for any reason, the most visible wallet is damaged, the hidden wallet and its main sources remain intact. With the help of the micro SD card, you can access it later.

Also, DigitalBitbox has two dual-factor authentication modes. First, in combination with another device, you can enable two-factor authentication to use the portfolio to create new transactions. You can also use DigitalBitbox as a second factor for another platform that uses two-factor authentication. It should be noted that this eliminates several other wallet options. Ideally, you should only use the first dual authentication mode if your DigitalBitbox is your primary hardware wallet. However, if you do not intend to perform a lot of transactions, this is a useful extended feature.

A New Competitor for Trezor and Ledger

Regarding the use of cryptocurrencies, if security is your priority, then DigitalBitbox is the hardware wallet you are looking for. It is effortless to communicate with and use open source applications for Linus, Mac, and Windows. The only real disadvantage for potential users is that it is currently limited to bitcoin. Otherwise, this is a new platform offering solid functionality and a very competitive price.

OpenDime Hardware Wallet

Recently, Bitcoin and other alternative currencies have generated a lot of enthusiasm. Understandably, some newcomers get the impression that Bitcoin is a sort of collector's item, but the fact is that Bitcoin is just a motto. Stripped of any hype and all the forecasts of value, Bitcoin is above all a means of exchange. OpenDime is a relatively new cold storage platform that includes the values of decentralization and relative anonymity. At a time when highly accessible, centralized, active exchanges are in fashion, OpenDime is reminiscent of a purer philosophy and is putting its new version of hardware portfolios on the market.

Cold Hard Bitcoin Sticks

OpenDime is known as the "piggy bank" of cold rooms in the world of cryptocurrencies. It works like other cold stores, with one exception: safe use for single use. This important difference changes a lot in the way people use it. Other storage platforms function more like portfolios that must be used repeatedly with a reasonable degree of security. While an OpenDime unit can be used extremely securely as an address to store Bitcoins until the owner has to withdraw money, but only once, in a direction parallel way when opening a piggy bank, an OpenDime storage unit can no longer be used with the same level of security once "open." OpenDime is a platform that converts Bitcoin's intangible assets into something physical that people can exchange with each other in the real world.

The Setup

OpenDime works the same way as most cold rooms. You buy it, you initialize it, and when you use it. The only addition to this process is that if you want to collect the money stored there, you have to open it literally.

The initialization process is relatively easy. Connect it to a USB port on your device. You must then generate a private key by adding 256 KB to the disk.

You can do this by dragging one or two random images. Once the private key is generated, the device is automatically ejected. Now he is ready to be used. To manage your resources and view your numeric address, you must open the index.htm file on the device. The user interface is easy to use and even offers links to various blockchain browsers.

Making Your Bit-Omlet

In the end, you want to have access to Bitcoins or Litecoins stored there. If you have the first version of OpenDime, you must break a plastic "tab" in the middle of the flash memory. Later versions work very much like resetting old routers. You must put a pen in a marked part of the device. Both processes physically change the disk. Then the private key associated with this OpenDime is downloaded to your PC or mobile device. This is the most vulnerable point when using OpenDime. Make sure to use a secure system for this. You can then use the private key to access your funds in the same way as with any other platform.

Security Risks and Hardware Wallets

Hardware wallets are safer than any other software wallet, such as a wallet running on your Android or iOS device, or a desktop computer. However, hardware wallets present uni⬚ue security risks that must be taken into account.

Tampering of the Device

It is always advisable to place an order directly to the hardware supplier. Indeed, someone can buy a computer hardware portfolio, manipulate it, and sell it used. They can program it to steal bitcoins or add a backdoor.

Most hardware wallets add some special tape to the package to make each manipulation more visible. This is another reason why it is recommended placing orders only with the hardware wallet company and not on a website such as eBay.

Bad Random Number Generator

Bitcoin private keys are based on cryptography. Random number generators, also called RNGs, are used to create private keys that protect bitcoins.

If the random number generator is not random enough, it means that someone else can easily recreate the private key of the hardware key. This attack occurred in the past with blockchain.info, a web wallet. More than 300 BTCs were lost because blockchain.info did not use a good RNG, so a hacker could again generate private keys and steal coins.

One way to avoid this is to use the modified word of the hardware portfolio. For example, with TREZOR, you can add a 25-word word to the 24-word seed. This means that you can technically add your RNG to the computer-generated RNG to make sure your private key is based on a good RNG.

What happens if the hardware wallet company goes out of business

All of the hardware wallets mentioned above work with other wallets. If the company's hardware wallet closes, then you can still use your wallet with another wallet, such as Electrum.

Suppose you are using TREZOR with TREZOR's myTREZOR wallet. TREZOR closes and is no longer compatible with the myTREZOR wallet and closes.

You can download Electrum on your computer in minutes. Once installed, you would set up your TREZOR, and all your transaction history and balance would be imported and identical. Indeed, Electrum uses the same seed of 24 words as that generated in the TREZOR configuration.

Which wallet can be used for each device?

Ledger Nano S, KeepKey, and TREZOR **work with:**

- Mycelium (Android version only)
- Electrum for Mac, Windows, and Linux
- GreenAddress

Do these hardware wallets work for Ethereum?

Yes, all of these wallets work with Ethereum, Litecoin, and many other currencies.

TREZOR and Ledger have published articles on their blog explaining their integration into various Ethereum wallets. The hardware wallet will tell you that you have to write the seed of 24 words on paper.

Should I take a picture of the seed with my phone as a backup?

No, no, and no!

Seeds generated by physical wallets can only be written. When you take a picture of your seed with a phone connected to the Internet, you place your entire wallet on a device connected to the Internet, which is easier for hackers. Please do not do that!

Why do the hardware wallets have buttons?

The buttons are used to confirm transactions. To send a transaction, you must physically maintain the buttons on the devices. This is a security feature. If a hacker had access to the hardware wallet, he still could not send TX without physical access to the buttons.

Do hardware wallets work with Coinbase?

One of the most fre□uently asked questions is how Coinbase works with hardware wallets.

It's a trap □uestion.

Coinbase does not work directly with a hardware wallet. However, you must send Coinbase bitcoins directly to your hardware portfolio as soon as you buy. Never store bitcoins for a long time in Coinbase or another exchange.

Too many people have already lost money in hacks like Bitfinex and Mount Gox.

So yes, you can use a hardware wallet with Coinbase. Buy from Coinbase then send it to a hardware wallet.

Also, this applies to ALL exchanges. Use Bitstamp? Yay! Once you have purchased bitcoins on Stamp, send the coins into your hardware wallet. The same applies to Kraken, Poloniex, or any other purse or service that contains your motto.

Note on hardware wallets.

Note that to use a Bitcoin/Cryptocurrency hardware wallet, you need a wallet of software to communicate with the device.

All hardware wallets have standard software portfolios designed by the company. However, you can also install a separate software portfolio to use the hardware portfolio with an alternative currency.

A simple example is that the TREZOR wallet itself supports Bitcoin, but you can also use Electrum to use your TREZOR with Bitcoin.

You may want to do this because Electrum has some unique features in TREZOR's wallet, such as creating specific outlets or "freezing" certain addresses so they can not be used.

Another important reason for installing other software wallets is to keep other unsupported tokens. For example, the standard Nano Ledger S software wallet may contain Ethereum, but possibly no other ERC20 token.

If you want to keep ERC20 tokens on the Nano S ledger, you need to install a third-party software wallet, such as MyEtherWallet (MEW). After installing MEW, you can register the ERC20 tokens on your Ledger Nano S.

There are several hundred ERC20 tokens. Downloading a software wallet can significantly increase the functionality of your hardware wallet.

Best Altcoin Hardware Wallets

If the use and investment in different cryptocurrencies are taken seriously, you have to buy a hardware wallet, possibly more than one. All financial instruments are intrinsically risky. Cryptocurrencies are generally more risky in many ways than most others. While it is impossible to eliminate all the risks when you use them, the hardware wallets contribute significantly to the reduction of most. However, not all hardware wallets are made the same way. Buying something is not enough, but you must carefully choose the right option for you. For years, cold storage options were rare, but they are more numerous than ever. In this book, let's take a look at the best in the market and why you should invest in it.

The Cool Wallet

Cool Wallet is a recent addition to the cold storage market and offers its interesting version. Its appearance remains in the first part of the brand, but given its form factor, it is more of a cryptographic credit card than a wallet.

Cool Wallet can also be compared reasonably with other cold storage devices. Also, the passphrases approach is unique compared to the standards of other hardware wallets. This device generates 20 random numbers instead of words and even gives you the option to send them to one of your devices. However, it is strongly recommended to write them.

Large wallets are also intrinsically verified for two reasons because they must be combined with another Bluetooth device to work. For some, this may be a potential security problem, but not a huge one, especially given the highly random "pass numbers" and the authentication process.

In terms of design, this is perhaps the best solution and is also an excellent backup hardware wallet for managing small amounts of cryptocurrencies.

Supports: Bitcoin, Bitcoin Cash, Ethereum, Litecoin, Ripple

DigitalBitbox

DigitalBitbox is one of the safest packages you can buy. Its physical interface has sacrificed a lot, but its software, independent of the open-source platform and its many functions, is doing well.

One of the best things about DigitalBitbox is the unprecedented change for password phrase and backups. This is perhaps the only device that exists, which in the worst-case comes with a simple but really "second chance." Also, it has several additional layers of security, including a hidden wallet and two-factor authentication.

It also helps to be one of the most affordable options available today. The only real disadvantage of DigitalBitbox is the lack of support for most altcoins. That said, if you only use Bitcoin primarily, this is the hardware portfolio.

Supports: Bitcoin

Ledger Nano S

Currently, the market leader in hardware wallets is the Ledger Nano S platform, and it is not difficult to understand why. This hardware wallet supports a large number of different cryptocurrencies and offers a wide range of security features.

Ledger's main competitor on the market is the original Trezor hardware portfolio. One of the main advantages of Ledger over Trezor is the freedom to create unique input phrases. The general ledger and the Trezor both need 20 passphrases for recovery and recovery; however, the Trezor package sends the user a random list. The Ledger gives the user the freedom to create their own. If aesthetics are important to you, the Ledger also has a design perhaps more elegant than Trezor.

The Ledger Nano S is a safe place to start with hardware wallets, especially if you only use a hot wallet. In many ways, it represents the "CoinBase.com" material portfolios. If you do not know where to start, it's probably something for you.

Support: Bitcoin, Bitcoin Cash, Bitcoin Gold, Ethereum, Classic Ethereum, Litecoin, DASH, Dogecoin, Ripples, Komodo, PoSW, ARK, Expanse, Ubiq, PIVX, Vertcoin, Viacoin, Neo, Stealthcoin, Stratos, Zcash

Trezor

Released when Bitcoin came out of its infancy, the Trezor was the first commercially available Bitcoin hardware wallet. Although many competitors have progressed over the years, it remains one of the best hardware wallets for cold storage of cryptocurrency.

As mentioned earlier, the general ledger is Trezor's main competitor for market dominance. Although the Ledger is newer and perhaps a bit more elegant, the Trezor finally has a better security record, as a JavaScript exploit recently been discovered that may affect it.

In a sense, Trezor is less "high-tech" than many other platforms; however, this makes it much less vulnerable. Another exciting feature of Trezor is the semi-double random factor pin generator that must be used before each use. By itself, it is resistant enough to any malware, but with this function, it is also protected against keyloggers.

Support: Bitcoin, Bitcoin Cash, Ethereum, Classic Ethereum, Litecoin, DASH, Dogecoin, Namecoin, Zcash, ERC-20 Tokens

Depending on your goals, your lifestyle, and your preferences, you can give preference to one or more of the listed material wallets. Notwithstanding which one you choose, you must choose at least one and use it. The security of your Bitcoins and other altcoins is in your hands.

Cryptocurrency Hardware Wallets

Hardware wallets are small devices that can be connected to your computer or phone. The hardware wallet securely generates your private keys in an offline environment. The innovation is that many wallets generate private keys on devices connected to the Internet, such as computers or mobile phones.

When you generate your private keys on an offline device, your keys are out of reach of hackers.

Pros:

- Private keys are not exposed to your computer
- Hardware wallets can not receive computer viruses or malware.
- You must have the hardware to confirm a transaction and prevent remote hacking.
- Most hardware wallets are encrypted with a PIN or other security feature.
- If you lose your hardware wallet, you can still collect your coins.

Cons:

- not free

In general, physical portfolios are the safest type of wallet. They have many built-in security features and support many kinds of cryptocurrency. If you want to store important encryption properties securely, consider purchasing a hardware wallet.

Cryptocurrency Software Wallets

Software portfolios cover different wallets, but in general, these are wallets that are downloaded or open numerically. These wallets include online/web portfolios, office wallets, and mobile wallets.

Each type of software wallet has different levels of security and accessibility, but hardware wallets are generally the safest but the most expensive option.

Due to the variety of software wallets, each type will be covered below in more detail.

Mobile Cryptocurrency Wallets

Mobile cryptocurrency wallets are wallets of software downloaded to your mobile device as an application. The application stores your cryptocurrency. These wallets are simple and easy to use and work well for people who pay for transactions with cryptocurrencies.

Mobile wallets are safer than online wallets, but they remain vulnerable to hackers.

Pros:

- Simple and easy to use.
- Ideal for people who often buy items with crypto-currencies.
- Some wallets have additional features such as QR code scanning or the use of near field communication technology.

Cons:

- Your wallet can be hacked, especially if your phone is permanently connected to the Internet.
- If someone steals your phone, you have access to your wallet.

Coinomi Mobile Wallet

Coinomi is another multi-cryptocurrency wallet available for iOS and Android.

Coinomi supports **currencies such as:**

- Bitcoin
- Dash
- Dogecoin
- Ethereum
- Ethereum Classic
- Litecoin
- Zcash

Coinomi is also integrated with ShapeShift and Changelly, another cryptocurrency exchange website.

Coinomi also offers a one-time backup. This feature allows you to create a backup phrase used to restore your private keys and access to all currencies.

Jaxx Mobile Wallet

Jaxx is a popular option for a multi-coin wallet for iOS and iPhone.

Jaxx supports several cryptocurrencies, **including:**

- Bitcoin
- Litecoin
- Ethereum
- Ethereum Classic
- Dash
- Zcash

The wallet is integrated with ShapeShift so that you can exchange coins of the wallet. Jaxx is also available for Android.

Cryptocurrency Wallets for Desktop

Desktop wallets are software wallets that are downloaded and installed on your computer. Your private keys are stored on your hard drive in these wallets. This makes them safer than web wallets. However, if your computer is connected to the Internet, your wallet remains vulnerable to attack.

Pros:

- You have your private keys, unlike a third party, which reduces your chances of hacking
- Desktop wallets are easy to use and offer a variety of functions.
- You can create a wallet for cold storage by disconnecting your computer from the Internet.

Cons:

- If your computer has access to the Internet, your wallet is more exposed.
- Your keys are stored offline. If your computer goes down, you risk losing your money.
- Regular backups are necessary to avoid the above
- If your computer is infected with viruses or malware, your wallet may have been hacked.

Using a desktop wallet provides more security than a Web wallet and several different functions. If you are planning to store large amounts of money in a desktop wallet, you should keep it in a cold store.

Exodus Wallet - Desktop Wallet

Exodus is another popular multi-cryptocurrency or universal wallet, which means that it supports many currencies. Like other office wallets, your private keys are stored on your computer.

Exodus is also integrated with ShapeShift so that you can trade your coins in your wallet.

Exodus supports the following **cryptocurrencies:**

- Bitcoin
- Litecoin
- Ethereum
- Dash

- Golem
- OmiseGO
- Decred, etc.

However, Exodus is not completely open-source, so it is not as reliable as an open-source wallet.

Atomic Wallet

Atomic Wallet is a new wallet with multiple currencies with which you can easily manage Bitcoin, Ethereum, XRP, and more than 300 coins and tokens.

Some of the best features of the **wallet are:**

- Encrypted private keys that never leave the user's device.
- Option to purchase crypto with a credit card in 20-30 minutes.
- Decentralized exchange of atomic exchanges included
- Immediate exchange through Changelly and Shapeshift.

Jaxx Desktop Wallet

Jaxx, the iOS and Android wallets mentioned above, is also available for the desktop. Jaxx is not open-source, but the code can be viewed on its website.

The desktop version supports the same currency as mentioned above and also incorporates ShapeShift. Jaxx saves your private keys on your computer.

Online Cryptocurrency Wallets

Online or web wallets are wallets accessible through your web browser. These portfolios store your private keys in the cloud. Exchange wallets such as Coinbase are a kind of web wallet.

With web wallets, you have quick access to your currency from any device connected to the Internet. However, since a business has private keys, you have no control over your wallet. These companies can use their private keys to steal their currency, or their servers can be hacked.

Pros:

- Direct access to your wallet
- Any Internet device can be used to access your currency.

Cons:

- You have no control over your private keys
- Companies can be hacked or steal their coins

You are advised to stay away from using web wallets as they are by far the least secure wallet. Do not store large sums of money in web wallets and do not use them for long-term storage.

MyEtherWallet - Online Ether and ERC20 Wallet

Pros:

- Integration with hardware wallets such as Ledger Nano S has made the Ledger Nano S + MEW combination the most popular way to store Ether and ERC20 tokens.
- Clear interface makes it easy to use new users, with or without a hardware wallet.

Cons:

- Without a hardware wallet, this is a web wallet, so it should not be used in large quantities

MyEtherWallet (MEW) is an open-source wallet launched in 2015. This software wallet is one of the most popular options for users wanting to store Ethereum tokens and other ERC20 tokens.

In particular, MyEtherWallet can not store Bitcoin, Bitcoin Cash, or other related currencies. Only for Ethereum parts.

MyEtherWallet locally generates private keys so that they are not stored on MEW servers. This increases security and puts the wallet in your hands.

Wallet Reviews and Guides

In the following section, some popular cryptocurrency wallets are presented.

MyEtherWallet (MEW) Guide

Making a MEW wallet is a relatively simple process. The first step is to visit the MyEtherWallet homepage. Make sure the domain of the website is exactly correct to prevent any falsification of the websites. Also, mark the website to avoid this problem in the future.

Enter a password on the home page and select the "Create a new wallet" button. MyEtherWallet generates a "KeyStore" file in UTC / JSON format. This is your password-protected private key.

Select the "Download KeyStore (UTC/JSON) File" button, then click "I understand.

The KeyStore file is downloaded, and you can see your private key on the next screen. You must save the KeyStore file to an offline hard drive or flash drive that you do not use online.

After clicking on "Save your address," you will be asked to unlock your wallet to display the address of your public wallet. Select "KeyStore/JSON File" in the selection screen.

Select the KeyStore file you saved previously, and enter the password that you originally used to create your wallet.

The advantage of using a KeyStore file is that you have not entered your complete private key, but only the password encrypted by the file. However, this process is not completely secure because you provide your private key file to a website.

A safer alternative is to use MyEtherWallet offline. It's a bit more complicated, but it may be worth the extra security. First, download, and then click "Etherwallet-vX.X.X.X.zip" to download and move the file to a flash drive.

Connect the USB flash drive to a computer without Internet access and extract all files from the drive to the computer. Select index.html in the MyEtherWallet folder to open the wallet.

This opens MyEtherWallet in your browser. You will be notified that you can not connect to the network, but this is normal. By using your wallet in this way, you can not see your Ether or other scales, but you can still see them with Etherscan.

Note: MyEtherWallet has recently been the target of significant hacking.

Exodus Wallet Step Guide

Start by visiting the Exodus website to set up an Exodus wallet. Select the "Download" button and choose your operating system.

Run the file you download and install the wallet. To fully configure your Exodus wallet, you must deposit a cryptocurrency.

Select the "Wallet" tab on the left side of the screen. Select the cryptocurrency you wish to deposit, then click "Receive." Your deposit address is displayed, and you can select the Copy button.

Open the exchange or wallet from which you are sending the cryptocurrency and paste the deposit address. After sending the cryptocurrency, you should be able to see it arrive in the Exodus wallet.

Select the "Backup" tab on your arrival. Create a password and continue. Exodus then reveals the 12-word recovery phrase that you can use to restore your crypto-currencies. Write this sentence and protect it.

Then create a backup link by entering your email address. You can follow this email link and enter your password to re-access your Exodus wallet.

With these security boxes installed, your wallet is defined.

Jaxx Desktop Wallet Guide

Jaxx, the iOS and Android wallets, as mentioned earlier, is also available for the desktop. Jaxx is not open-source, but the code can be viewed on its website.

The desktop version supports the same currency as mentioned above and also incorporates ShapeShift. Jaxx stores your private keys on your computer.

To set up a Jaxx wallet for the desktop, first go to your website and select the download tab. Select the desktop version.

Once the wallet is downloaded and installed, the first screen with the release notes. Select "continue" and accept the terms of use. On the next screen, select "Create a new wallet" and continue. Then, select the custom option because it allows you to configure security features and other preferences.

You can then select the cryptocurrency wallet (s) you want to create. You must select at least one, but you can add or remove others at any time. You will then be asked to select the fiat currency. The value of your coins appears in this currency.

Jaxx will ask you if you want to create a wallet now. Select Yes to generate a 12-word save phrase. Write it down as the other backups and keep it in a safe place.

You will then be prompted to write your backup phrase on the Jaxx Wallet to ensure that the step will not be ignored.

Finally, you can configure 4-digit security that gives you regular access to your wallet.

Frequently Asked Questions

This section is intended to answer the most common questions about cryptocurrency wallets.

Which wallet is best for me?

The cryptocurrency wallet that's right for you depends on how you use it.

If you only need a wallet for some small and infrequent payments, it would be useful to use one of the wallets above for Android, iPhone, or a desktop.

If you invest in encrypted currencies and need secure storage, a wallet of hardware such as Ledger or TREZOR will better meet your needs.

What about paper wallets?

Paper wallets are an inexpensive way to create secure storage for cryptography. The biggest problem is that it is very confusing and difficult to do well. If you want to use a paper wallet, you can make research yourself on Google.

How do I add funds to my wallet?

You must first purchase cryptocurrency in exchange and then transfer the exchanged coins into your wallet. This is the only way to fund your wallet.

With some wallets, you can buy bitcoins on the wallet, but there is no wallet yet to buy a coin other than Bitcoin.

Is Coinbase a good wallet?

Coinbase is an exchange and cannot be used as a wallet. Coinbase is certainly a reliable place to buy bitcoins, but as soon as you do, move Bitcoin, Litecoin, or Ether to one of the wallets described in this book.

Is Robinhood a good wallet?

Robinhood is not a Bitcoin wallet. You cannot withdraw your coins from their app.

How do I get a cryptocurrency address?

Your wallet automatically generates addresses for you. Each crypto has slightly different formats for addresses.

Bitcoin addresses start with 1 or 3 and look **like this:**

- *1BvBMSEYstWetqTFn5Au4m4GFg7xJaNVN2*
- *3J98t1WpEZ73CNmQviecrnyiWrn⬚RhWNLy*

Ethereum addresses start with a 0 and usually look **like this:**

- *0xde0B295669a9FD93d5F28D9Ec85E40f4cb697BAe*

Litecoin addresses start with an L and usually look **like this:**

- *LVXXmgcVYBZAuiJM3V99uG48o3yG89h2Ph*

How do I open a cryptocurrency account?

There is no cryptocurrency account. You can have a wallet where your coins are stored.

You can create an account in a cryptocurrency exchange, but it is not a standard cryptocurrency account the same way you have a bank account.

Any common mistakes to be careful of?

The biggest mistake here people committing is the money trade. Then, the exchange is hacked, or exit scam and people lose their money.

DO NOT STORE YOUR MONEY ON AN EXCHANGE!

Cryptocurrency Security Advice

This section gives you some tips for protecting your cryptocurrency in a variety of ways, whether you're in a purse or wallet.

Value migration to the digital sphere poses new challenges in the area of best security practices. As with any unit of value, there is always someone, somewhere, who tries to obtain that value for their ends, whether through coercion, social manipulation, or brute force.

This manual is intended to provide an overview of best practices for protecting your encryption resources. Although most of these steps are not mandatory, tracking them increases your financial security and peace of mind in the world of cryptocurrencies.

Passwords - Complexity & Re-use

From scratch, the complexity of the password and reuse are two important critical points that many average users do not see well. As you can see in this list, the average complexity of the password leaves something to be desired. The less complex your password, the more difficult it is to hack into your account if you use the same passwords or even small variations of the same passwords in different accounts, your chances of compromise increase dramatically.

So what can you do? Fortunately, the solution is relatively simple. Use 14 randomly generated characters and passwords and never use the same password again. If this sounds daunting, consider using a password manager such as LastPass or Dashlane to help you generate and save passwords.

Here you can check if an account linked to you has been compromised here and use this tool to test the strength of the variations of your passwords (do not use your real password here, only structured variants).

Dedicated Email Accounts

Almost all online services/exchanges require some link between email accounts during the activation process. If it's like most people, you're probably using the standard email you've had for years, and you can add a slightly more complex password to the account itself.

However, in most cases, hackers only have access to their e-mail to reset their account passwords. It's as easy as navigating the site/swap and clicking on the "I forgot my password" link to start the process. So, if you are like most people and have an email address that has been active for years, with a weak login password, your chances of being hacked are much greater.

For the reasons above, do yourself a favor and create a new email/dedicated email address to use with your encrypted accounts. Services such as ProtonMail and Tutanota are free and offer end-to-end encryption without sacrificing usability (availability of mobile applications, etc.). If you decide to continue using Gmail, consider enabling Google's advanced security program.

Two-Factor Authentification

In general, it is recommended that you configure 2-factor authentication (2FA) for each account that offers this feature, even if the service is not encryption-related. The only thing 2FA asks for is a second confirmation that you are who you are when you sign in to the accounts. This is usually something you know (password) and something you own (SMS code sent to the phone).

Although SMS remains the most common form of 2FA offered by online services, it is, unfortunately, the least secure. **The following 2FA methods for general use are ranked safer unless:**

1. **FIDO U2F:** This is a physical device that connects to a USB port, and that re?uires physical pressure on the button to generate a uni?ue 2FA access code. It is better because a hacker must have the device physically in his possession to access his account. Most hacks take place remotely, making it our best 2FA option (although it is not a panacea).

2. **Google Authenticator:** An application that resides on your mobile device and browses one-time access tokens. If you follow this

route, you must register the backup code specified in the initial configuration. If you do not have it and your phone is lost or broken, you can not restore the configuration of this code.

3. **Authy:** Similar to Google Authenticator, but perhaps less secure, because you can regain access to codes from another mobile device if your primary device is lost or damaged (this feature can be disabled but is enabled by default). While this may seem ideal, a little more convenient for you is also more convenient for those who are trying to hack it.

4. **SMS:** the codes are sent to your mobile phone by SMS. Better than no 2FA at all, but subject to social engineering attacks SIM. Curiously, the vulnerabilities of SMS 2FA only appeared when the popularity of Bitcoin began to grow.

Secure Crypto Storage

If you do not have a private key, you do not have your money.

This category is the way most people have been compromised and lost money in cryptography. How to primarily manage an exchange (Coinbase, Binance, Bittrex, Poloniex, etc.) as a portfolio to store your encryption resources.

Mount Gox, Bitfinex, BitGrail, and Coincheck are just four of the few cryptographic exchanges that have been hacked over the past five years, with a stolen amount of more than $ 1 billion. Although some users of these exchanges have improved to a certain extent, many still suffer from the partial or total loss of the cryptographic funds they had at the time of the attacks.

An advice is to store cryptography on wallets of material or paper that you manage alone. If you want to trade on the stock exchange, do it with funds that you might want to lose completely in case the stock market or your account is compromised.

Ledger, Trezor, and Keepkey are among the recommended gear carriers manufacturers. As with any hardware/software, you must ensure that the firmware of your device is up-to-date because patches are constantly being removed to resolve security issues.

Mobile Crypto Wallet

Wallets for mobile applications such as Mycelium, Breadwallet, Samourai, Cryptonator, etc. They must be treated in the same way as your physical wallet.

Only hold small amounts of discretionary spending funds in these portfolios because they are more susceptible to lose or theft. Again, what is more, convenient for you is also for a malicious actor. Your phone is also exposed to malware and should not be considered safe enough to store large amounts of money.

Phishing Attacks

If you have cryptography, you are an ideal target for phishing. Facebook and Twitter are just two of the many paths taken by hackers to look for potential victims. It has become common to see fake emails for encryption exchange or to circulate fundraising confirmations to the ICO, as in the example below.

A phishing email that looks like Blockchain.info. Note the delivery address and the irregularity of the logo.

It is best to NEVER open suspicious attachments or provide login information by email and always check the logo, wording, and address of each mail belonging to the financial accounts or requesting confidential information.

If in doubt, access the legitimate exchange or web service from which the email is suspected and contact your support team to find out if what you have received is valid before taking additional action.

Clean Hardware

This is the general best practices section of this guide. Malware is ubiquitous on the Internet, and whatever your attention to detail, you will likely sooner or later be a victim of malicious software. As such, it is best to have active antivirus subscriptions on your devices and perform periodic scans. I like running Malwarebytes and Roguekiller on my PC once a week, and I have background analytics on my phone that runs automatically. In general, Windows is the least secure operating system, mainly because it is the oldest and most dominant operating system in use today. Many security experts prefer Linux or iOS.

Web security is similar to a whack-a-mole game, and your level of security will likely increase with the amount of confidential (or crypto-assets) data you protect.

Although there is no "inaccessible" system, you can take steps to reduce your risk of compromise significantly.

Always remember:

- Use complex and unique passwords
- Create a separate/dedicated email account for encryption services
- Use two-factor authentication
- Store most (if not all) of your funds in physical wallets
- Be careful with phishing emails
  Good luck, and be careful.

What is a Block and How is it Made?

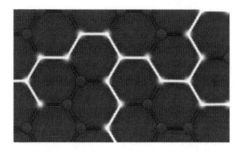

Now let's focus on the blockchain and how it's made. There are a lot of different parts that come with the blockchain. It is a complicated piece of technology that has really made a difference in how Bitcoin and other cryptocurrencies run, in addition to changing up a wide variety of other industries. But one of the most fundamental parts of the blockchain, the block, is at the heart of how this technology works.

The structure of the block

The best place to get started here is with the structure of the block. A block is basically going to be a container data structure. When it comes to the world of Bitcoin, this block can contain more than five hundred transactions on average. This can add up to a lot of transactions for the regular user, and unless you are doing day trading or selling a ton of products with your online store, it could take you many months to fill up the block while on the network.

Of course, with other applications of the blockchain, you may find that there is a differing amount of transactions that are held on the block. This number is going to depend on how the platform was set up. But for the Bitcoin network that originally uses blockchain, it is 500 transactions on average.

Now, there are some changes in the size of the block based on whether you are using Bitcoin or Bitcoin Cash. In the original Bitcoin network, the block was about 1 MB, but in Bitcoin Cash, the block has been expanded to 8 MB. This is important to the Bitcoin Cash network because it allows more transactions to be processed every second.

To keep things simple, a block is composed of a header as well as a long list of transactions. Let's look at how each of these work by starting out with the header.

The block header

So, the first thing that we are going to talk about with the block is the block header. This block header is going to contain the metadata about this block. There are three main types of metadata that can be shown which includes:

The block hash from the previous block: Remember that when you are working with the blockchain, each block is going to inherit from the block ahead of it. This is because you need to use the hash from the previous block to create a new hash on this new block. So, for each new block N, we will feed it the hash of the block N-1.

Mining competition: The next part is known as mining competition. For a block to join the main blockchain on the network, it must be given a hash that is recognised as valid. This is going to contain the timestamp, the difficulty, and the nonce. Therefore mining is so important because it provides all of these to the blocks so that they can stay on the blockchain and be accounted for.

Merkle tree root: This third part is going to be the data structure that can be used to summarise the transactions in the block.

The block identifiers

There are also a number of block identifiers that are important to the system as well. To help you identify a block, you can use a cryptographic hash. A good way to look at this is like a digital signature of the block. This is going to be created by hashing the block header using the algorithm SHA256.

Remember here that we will use a second hash in order to create our first one. This is because each block is going to rely on the hash from the previous block to construct a new one that it can use. The block hash is going to have a unique identifier. For this system to work, you are never going to find two blocks that have the same hash.

There is another way that you can identify a specific block, and this is by looking at the block height. The block height is going to be the position of a block inside of the blockchain. So, if you have a block that is in the 500312 position, it means that there are going to be 500311 blocks that occur in the blockchain before this one.

This one is going to be a little bit different. The block height is not going to be unique. It is possible that a few blocks could compete to have the same position. This often happens when you are dealing with a hard fork in the system, such as when Bitcoin Cash came out.

What are Merkle Trees?

The transactions that occur on each block are going to be contained inside a structure that is known as either a Binary-Hash tree or a Merkle Tree. This is sometimes difficult to understand, so we are going to spend time looking at some examples and some coding to see how it works.

A Merkle tree is going to be constructed when you are recursively hashing pairs of nodes, which are transactions when working with cryptocurrency, until there ends up being only one hash. This is going to be known as a root or the Merkle root. If we decide to stay in the world of Bitcoin, the algorithm that we use to make up this hash is going to be SHA256, and you will apply it twice each time.

Let's look at an example of how this works. We are going to have a block that has four transactions. To keep things simple, we are going to give each transaction a string like what you see below:

const tA = 'Hello'
const tB = 'How are you?'
const tC = 'This is Thursday'
const tD = 'Happy new Year'

Now, it is not going to matter how many transactions go into each block on this network; they will be summarised with a 32-byte hash. One thing to note here is that the Merkle tree is going to be considered a binary tree. This means that if there ends up being an odd number of transactions that come on the block, the system is going to duplicate the last one so that you end up with an even number. Then you will be able to construct the tree.

Because each of the leaves that are in this tree will need to depend on the leaves that come before it, you can imagine that it is pretty much impossible to alter just one leaf of this without altering the others. Just by changing up one of these leaves, or one transaction when working with Bitcoin, the hash is going to change.

The Merkle tree can help in several ways. First, it ensures that you are using the right leaves together. The Merkle root is not going to work out if you try to tamper with the transactions or use the wrong parts. Alternatively, if someone tries to get onto the network and alter what is going on in the chain, then it is going to change the root as well. This can end up making a clutter with a longer blockchain and is thus, one of the ways that the users can ensure that the network is not being messed with.

Users are also able to prove whether a transaction that is in a block is supposed to be there. This is a great way to keep some of the transparency intact within the network. You can do this by creating what is known as either a Merkle path or an Authentication path. The only thing that you will need to know in order to do this is the log base 2(N) 32-byte hash.

If we are looking at the four transactions that we talked about above in the Merkle tree, you would just need to write out the equation log base 2(4) = 2 =>. If you have a path of two hashes for a tree of four transactions, this is going to prove that a transaction belongs to the Merkle tree you are working in.

You can do this no matter how many transactions are present in the Merkle tree. Let's say that you want to look to see if this works when there are sixteen transactions on the tree. You would just use the same equation that we did before but replace the N with 16 instead. So, the equation that you would use is log base 2(16) = 4 =>. If you have a path here that has four hashes for a tree of 16 transactions, you will be able to use this equation to prove that a specific transaction is supposed to be a part of that Merkle tree.

You can also do this with any amount that you would like to do. For example, using the equation log base 2(1500) = 10.55 => will help you if you have a path of eleven hashes for a tree with 1500 transactions. You could use the transaction above to show that this transaction belongs to the Merkle tree.

The block is crucial in making sure that the blockchain works. It is basically going to be able to hold onto all the information that comes with the transactions that users complete on the network. These transactions could include money, like with the Bitcoin network, or some other transaction of value based on how the blockchain is being used.

How do Blockchain Components Interact?

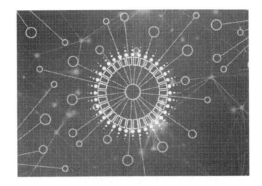

So, now that we have spent some time talking about Blockchain and some of the benefits that come with this technology, it is now time to understand how this type of technology is going to work. It is simple for users to use this kind of technology; it only takes a few minutes to do transactions and you are signed up automatically when you join in on a digital currency. But the things that happen behind the scenes are a bit more complex, which helps to provide the trust and security that the system needs.

Since we will mostly associate blockchain with Bitcoin and some of the other digital currencies that are out there, it is easiest to look at how the blockchain will work on these networks. It will work similarly on other networks as well, but this will help to keep things in order. On the blockchain, when you complete a transaction, it will end up showing up, in order, on one of the blocks you are using. When the block is filled up, it will join in the permanent record and will link together with the other blocks that you have completed in order to form a chain. This all works together to help keep your information in order and keeps it secure from others who may want to look at the data.

Each block in the blockchain is going to be responsible for holding onto all the vital information about the transactions that you complete and each of the blocks will hold onto a lot of data. Depending on the network that you work with, these blocks could contain information about currencies, digital rights, identity, and property titles to name a few. Since these blocks can hold onto so much information and will keep that information safe, the blockchain is one of the best ways to help people interact, send money, and even make their purchases.

When you decide to join the Bitcoin network, and you create your Bitcoin address, you will join in on its blockchain. Each user will receive a block that they will be able to fill up each time that they finish a new transaction. These blocks can hold onto quite a bit of information, and some people will fill them up quickly while others may take a bit longer.

After the block has been filled up with the different transactions that you are working on, they are going to become a part of the permanent record on Bitcoin. You will be able to look at this any time that you want and make sure that everything is in place and no one is messing around with the system. Then, they will join the Bitcoin network's blockchain, and you will start making your own personal blockchain, which will just contain all the blocks that carries your own transactions.

When one block is all filled up, it is time to receive another block, which the system will send over to you automatically. There is a specified number of transactions that can be added to each block so some people will get done filing them up faster than others based on how busy they are on the network. You can then start to fill up that block with transactions as well, and the process keeps going for as long as you keep using the network. Every user on the Bitcoin network, or whatever platform you are using at the time, will have their own blockchain that is full of personal transactions. But as the blocks fill up, those will be added to the permanent blockchain that the Bitcoin network relies on, so the information is kept safe. This process works together to make sure that the Bitcoin network remains transparent to use.

This can all seem a little bit confusing right now, but one way to think about how the blockchain works is to think of it as your own bank statement. Each block that you receive will be like a monthly statement that you get from the bank. You can look it over to see what transactions you have completed in recent times and check to make sure it is all good.

After you have finished a few of these statements, they will all become part of your bank history. They will be a part of your permanent record with the bank (or regarding the blockchain, with the Bitcoin network), and you can always look back to see what payments you made, what funds you received, and any other transaction. The main difference between these is that the blockchain is going to be online and will only oversee things that happen on the Bitcoin network.

One nice thing that comes with the Blockchain technology is that it works with Bitcoin to keep your transactions safe and secure. There are some unique codes or some hashes that will be added in so that hackers and other people won't be able to steal your information. Anyone who is on the network can see these transactions, but they will have to look through these special hashes to see what is going on. It is the work of the miners on the Bitcoin network that will make sure the blockchain ledger is secure, and they will be rewarded with 25 Bitcoins each time they are successful.

The job of the miner may sound easy, but there are some complications that can come with it and they are in charge of maintaining most of the security of this system. They will need to come up with the unique hashes that will help to hide up all your information so that it will be safe from others who want to look. However, they can't just go through and write out any random number that they like, or anyone could do this, and all the coins on Bitcoin would be mined.

Instead, there are a few rules to the hashes that are created. First, the beginning of each hash needs to have a certain number of zeroes, and since you don't know how a hash will look until you are done, you could create quite a few of these before getting results. Also, the hashes must be designed so that if any one character in the chain is changed, it is going to change up all the characters that come after it as well. This makes it complicated to make a good hash, but it does make it easier to catch if someone has been messing around in the blockchain.

The mining process can be really rewarding if you are good at it, but it takes a lot of time and patience. Moreover, as the network becomes more popular and more of the coins are released, the harder the work becomes to get the hashes that are needed. Therefore it is important to really calculate how much you will make from the mining process compared to how much you will spend if you want to get into mining. With Bitcoin, it takes up so much computing power, and there is so much competition now, that many people are not interested in doing this at all. They would end up spending more than they would make when they get done with the costs of this endeavour.

As you can guess, the process of creating one of these codes is not the easiest, but these rules ensure that your information is going to stay safe and that not just anyone could add in a random code to the mix. If they could do that, then a code could do the work and the security would be gone. The amount that the rewarded Bitcoins are worth will vary depending on what time it is and how much value the world has placed on these coins. Since the current value is a little over $9000, you could end up making a bit of money in the process while helping the network do well. Of course, you could spend a lot of money with computing power as well, so figure that out ahead of time.

The blockchain is an elegant piece of technology that has so many potential applications for users to enjoy. Right now, it is the leading force that has helped Bitcoin become so popular, but it is sure to change many other aspects of our world in the future. It is such a simple idea, just a ledger to keep track of transactions, but it is so efficient and easy to use that many platforms for different applications are already in use on the blockchain.

What Problems does the Blockchain Solve?

While Blockchain Technology is still relatively new, there are many people who are exploring what it would be able to do in the future. There have already been so many ways that the blockchain can solve some of our modern problems that it is likely to keep on going and won't take long until it can be implemented in many areas of our world. This chapter will explore the different problems that the blockchain can solve.

Solve security problems

Experts agree that there is some validity to thinking that 'blockchain technology' could help to solve many of the security issues that occur today in banking. The blockchain is known as a distributed file system where each participant who joins the network will be able to keep copies of the file, and if there are any changes to it, there must be a consensus before this happens. These files are composed of blocks, and each one is going to contain the cryptographic signature from the block that occurred ahead of it. This helps to create an immutable record and will verify the integrity of each transaction.

According to the vice president of Greenwich Associates, nobody has been able to hack onto the blockchain that is with Bitcoin and steal Bitcoins. This shows that the blockchain is a very secure piece of technology. It is based off some strong cryptography that keeps all the transactions secure. When an asset has been digitised on this blockchain, then, cryptography has been used to help identify and secure ownership of the asset. The only way that people can steal or make a copy of any digital asset is if they have the private key that can unlock the cryptography that is on the asset. This helps to keep it much more secure than what conventional banks are using.

It is usually pretty hard to steal these private keys. This is because most people who are using the blockchain, or the cryptocurrencies that utilise the blockchain, will use a wallet to keep the currency and the private keys safe. These wallets are secure software programs that are designed to keep the coins, and the information about the user, as safe as possible.

As discussed, some wallets are even more secure than before. These are multi-signature wallets which will require more than one person who must sign a transaction before the blockchain executes it. This helps to add on more protection to the coins that are used. Some people take it even a step further and will store their assets as well as the private keys in cold storage so that they are not connected to the internet.

While it is still possible that the wallet could be hacked and that someone could get a hold of your security key and your coins, this method has proved to be much safer compared to working with modern banks. There is a lot less fraud out there, and it is less likely that your information could be stolen. Many banks could benefit from using the blockchain for purchases so fraud and hacking would become less likely.

Speed up transactions

With the methods that we currently adopt, transactions are slow. Each bank must go through and reconcile the transactions that they are doing. Once someone makes a purchase, the first bank must go through and deduct that money from their own ledgers. And then the bank responsible for receiving the money will have to do the same thing in order to add the money to their ledger.

This process takes much time and can add a ton of fees to the whole thing as well. It is common to see a transaction take three to five days to finish. In modern times where the purchase can take just a few minutes to complete, it can be frustrating to wait several days or more just to get the transaction to complete because of how slow the bank can be.

With the blockchain, you do not run into this issue as much. The blockchain is one ledger that everyone can use at the same time. You do not need to reconcile things on more than one ledger, allowing for the transactions to get done much quicker; sending money to anyone you want. With the traditional Bitcoin ledger, you can get the transaction done within ten minutes. With Litecoin and some of the other ledgers, you could get the transaction done in two and a half minutes.

Many banks are seeing the benefit of using these systems to help their customers. They realise how much their customers would like to see their transactions get done quickly and how much time and money it would save themselves in the process.

Sending money anywhere you want

Another benefit of using the blockchain is that you would be able to handle sending money to anyone they want, no matter where they reside. With our traditional methods of using a bank or a financial institution, doing this could take at least several days to complete and then there are a lot of fees that are added to the whole thing. This can make sending money to friends and family in other countries, or even purchasing items in other countries, hard to do.

It seems so outdated to not be able to interact better with people in all parts of the world. We are used to being able to travel, talk, shop, and more with people no matter where they are located. But most current financial companies are more interested in going through and reconciling their ledgers and charging money to do these things. This has greatly inhibited trade throughout between various countries.

With the blockchain, this is no longer a big issue. The blockchain is just one ledger, so that can help save a lot of time and hassle. Since the ledger is the same for any member connected to the network, it takes the same amount of time, and money, to send assets to any part of the world. It does not matter whether you send the money to someone no matter where they live without the wait time or the extra costs.

Helps solve big problems in social media

There are a number of ways that the blockchain would be able to help solve some of the significant problems that occur in social media. Many people consume social media on several different platforms including LinkedIn, Pinterest, Instagram, Facebook, and Twitter. It is most likely that people will use several of these, instead of just one. Most of these networks are going to rely on a business model that runs on ads.

There is an issue with this for everyone. Platforms, creators, and users are going to be compensated unequally for how they participate on the platform. For example, President Obama produced the most liked tweet in the history of Twitter, but he never received a reward in doing this. But with the help of a private ledger, such as what is found on the Ethereum blockchain, it would be easier for companies to track how users interact with their content. This would help the company to quantify their worth to the network and can lead the way to them being properly compensated for the activity that they do on that network.

Also, in-app currencies that are supported by this 'blockchain technology' could really restructure how users start to consume content socially. While there are some companies, such as Rize, that are trying to restructure their social media model, then making use of a social media company called Kik is one of the most popular options for doing this. For example, this company (Kik) just launched a new cryptocurrency, which is known as Kin, and raised almost $100 million in ICO.

The point of Kin is to offer an incentive for network contributors and developers to bring their services and applications to that network, without needing an intermediary. The long-term vision of this is to create a new in-app marketplace where brands can advertise to their users with the help of chat, and collect payment, while users can sell services to others with the app. While it is not a surefire way to success because it could bring in investors who will just want to make money on the volatility of the market, rather than to contribute, it could be the start of growing content on social media and ensuring that people are being compensated properly for the work that they are doing.

Blockchain could help with fake news

Fake news has become a big problem in our modern world. With the easy spread of information, the ease of being able to start up a website, and the relatively hard work of proving a source, it is easy for someone to get online and just write what they would like about any topic. There have been a lot of spoofs out there, from things famous people did and said, to hearing about cryptocurrencies crashing and more.

There are a number of reasons why fake news is bad. First, it is a huge opportunity cost. This is because if someone is raising fake news on purpose that a certain cryptocurrency is rising, and then a ton of people purchase it because they believe that the coin is worth something, then there is an opportunity cost, as well as actual losses when that coin is found to be bad.

In some cases, the fake news can be malicious. It can be against someone or a group of people. It can really harm a business, a person, and even a country. In some cases, it can be used to help incite racial hatred as well.

And of course, there is the also the issue of fake news taking away important attention from legitimate news sources. If you get to choose between an article stating that that Bitcoin is going to fall a bunch in the next few months, compared to one that discusses how well Bitcoin is doing. The first one will often have a better title and get more views, so it will do better.

The blockchain will be able to help with this. The news portal will need to run on this network, but it will ensure that the news is on a decentralised system that will rely on the wisdom of the crowd and the people who value news that is high-quality. It can help to generate some more trust in the news that you read, rather than allowing people to write what they like. Moreover, it would not need to be run by a government, which makes it more trustworthy.

This kind of platform would have people use a token in order to pay for news that is high-quality. Users and even advertisers on this system would be able to rate the content that they see, based on an upvote and downvote system. It could even allow some independent fact-checkers who will check the content that is on the system, and they can then receive rewards for their work on the blockchain.

If some of the news on the network were seen to be inaccurate, the karma points of the person who posted them would be affected. This helps to promote better quality rather than allowing people to post anything that they like. The news portal will be on a blockchain that is open sourced and can show up on the news feed of the user, allowing the portal to be immutable, open to the scrutiny of the public, and transparent.

Can help with copyright issues

Keeping track of the copyright that comes with photography and other works of art can be hard. With the expansion of the internet, it is easy for people all around the world to steal your photos and use them the way that they would like. Whether these are personal pictures, or you want to sell them to earn some money, this can be a problem. The blockchain can help with this.

Thanks to a new program known as COPYTRACK that was released in 2014, photographers can help figure out when copyright infringement takes place. While pursuing this kind of problem is hard to do and way too costly, COPYTRACK provides you with the tools that you need to search and match how some images are doing throughout the world. Even if some changes have occurred to the image, whether they are flipped, edited, or cropped, these tools can help the picture to be found. Once the owner of the picture detects that their image was stolen, they can simply click and then submit a claim to the COPYTRACK program. COPYTRACK will offer legal enforcement or post-licensing without risk or any hassle on the part of the person who took the picture. This is a worldwide service that also has lawyers present to help. If you are successful, the program will take a commission off what you make.

So, how does this work with the blockchain? The rights owner will be able to use the blockchain that comes with COPYTRACK to authenticate themselves. Then they can go through and upload their images to be certified. Once the blockchain has approved this, all the data is going to be secured using the hashes in the blockchain. From here on out, those images are going to be tracked all the time for how they are used online. This can also check the licensing information and the payments that are given for the pictures that are stored on this blockchain for you.

Basically, this is going to allow you to get full transparency to the market for image licensing. It also helps you to get control back to your pictures and makes it harder for people to take your pictures and use them the way that they want without paying you for your work.

As you can see, there are many solutions that the blockchain can help with; whether you are dealing with the online banking world, helping with transparency in many different markets, or even helping with the copyright mixture, and so much more.

What Started the Blockchain Revolution?

The Blockchain Revolution, as well as Bitcoin, came at the perfect time. There were many things going on around the world and in the economy that were making people worried and mad about the way that their money worked. They did not like how the economic downturn occurred. They did not like that they couldn't seem to trust the financial institutions and governments who were supposed to keep their money safe. It was time for a change.

Bitcoin and the 'blockchain technology' that came with it, came out during a time when people were fed up. Many countries throughout the world were in turmoil with a recession and inflation was at an all-time high. Many governments were not able to control the money, and a lot of inflation and corruption were happening, both in the government and in many banks. Big companies were getting bailed out for their improper use of money, but many of the common people were being stuck with the bill. And because the recession lasted for so long, many people grew weary of the system that was already in place and wondered if there was a better way.

Because of the recession and the disillusionment with the system at that time, Bitcoin was poised to take off. Many speculate whether Bitcoin and other cryptocurrencies would have had the same success if they were released at some other time in history. It seemed that the economy and the perceptions of most people at this time made these currencies perfect and helped them to take off at a rate that they would never have been able to do before.

Thanks to the blockchain, there was now a solution that everyone could be happy with. The blockchain allowed for a new currency to work well, one that did not have to rely on the government or any other central authority. It worked based off a mathematical equation, and the only way that more coins could be released is due to the work of the miners, not because someone was messing around in it.

The blockchain offered transparency. You could always go and look at your own transactions and the transactions of anyone in the network. Fraud was kept to a minimum because most of the computers on the network had to agree before any changes in the blockchain could happen. Considering that there are computers connected to the Bitcoin network all over the world, it is almost impossible for someone to make unauthorised changes to the blockchain.

It also added security, something that is sorely missing in our current financial world. The miners work to keep the information about your transactions as private as possible, adding unique hashes to each block of code to ensure that it is hard to read through. Everything also lines up with the blocks that occur before it, making it hard for anything to be messed with without anyone noticing.

All of this and more helped to make Bitcoin, and then the Blockchain, a powerful tool that brought on the 'blockchain revolution'. People were no longer reliant on their government to handle the money they used. They could stay safe online and exchange money anywhere in the world, and it would all be safe and secure on the blockchain ledger. For the first time in history, one could control their own money, without risk of fraud, stolen money, or high inflation, without the help of the government.

Even though a lot of the mainstream is still trying to play some catchup, the blockchain revolution has been underway for some time. Moreover, this revolution is taking the world by storm. It has already made big changes in global finances, computer science, data sciences, and business just to name a few.

This may seem like a big claim. There are many people who may have just heard about cryptocurrencies and the blockchain for the very first time, and they may have a hard time verifying this information. Even as Bitcoin, as well as other altcoins, keep topping themselves each week on the market, and there are new ICOs that introduce more exciting technologies all the time, it is still possible to keep up with all the changes, as long as you are dedicated to doing so.

The 'blockchain revolution' in financial services

Financial institutions are naturally the first ones to look at how the blockchain revolution can influence them. They work in a similar manner and would need a blockchain platform that is like what is found on Bitcoin. The current banking system is flawed. It is rife with lots of fraud and many times the transactions that you do on this will take several days to complete. In our fast-paced world, this is unacceptable.

The biggest issue that comes with the financial industry right now is that it costs these financial institutions so much to do their work. It is estimated that the blockchain could help to reduce the infrastructure costs for these banks for securities trading, cross-border payments, and regulatory compliance by $15 to $20 billion each year by 2022. And some experts believe that this figure is too low.

This is a huge amount of savings for most banks, especially the larger ones that are dealing with some of the issues above. It is savings that would allow them to pass on that money to their customers and even to open new products and make more profit. Many large financial institutions who can afford it or who can work with other companies to share the platform are already working to see how the blockchain can help them out.

In addition, this 'blockchain technology' can revolutionise the transaction process because it will disperse the control of the money and can provide the customer with complete transparency. This helps to reduce the need for a middleman or authorized person that must verify all the transactions. This helps to add some more trust and reduces the fraud and other issues that can come up because the blockchain can do all the work.

The best part is that the blockchain can be used in so many other areas rather than just with cryptocurrencies. It has many ways that it could transform how government and businesses work. It can record and track all these details about a transaction or about who owns an asset. It can help to automate contracts and will simplify this process in no time.

As you can see, there are a ton of different reasons that this blockchain revolution can make a difference in how our government and our financial world will work in the future. People are tired of all the red tape and the fraud that can go on with our traditional banking industry. This eliminates that, provides more security, gets rid of the middleman, and still provides the transparency that people are looking for.

The blockchain revolution has really changed up a lot of things in our world. No longer are we necessarily dependent on the government to control our money. No longer do we have no control over our money or must wait forever for a transaction or pay much money to send something overseas. The blockchain has been able to open many doors for our currencies, and in other areas, and it is likely to keep moving into the future with many more changes to come.

Why are Current Financial Services Disrupted?

The current financial world moves millions of dollars every day and can work with billions of people throughout the world. Despite helping so many people, this system has been rife with problems. It has added many costs for businesses and individuals through fees and delays. It has caused friction through onerous and redundant paperwork, and there is a lot of crime and fraud that is out there. In fact, forty-five percent of financial intermediaries, such as money transfer services, stock exchanges, and payment networks already suffer from lots of economic crime each year, but higher than what was found in other industries.

All these issues bring up the question, why is the financial system that we use so inefficient? First, the problem comes with the system being antiquated. Even though it has tried to catch up to the modern world, it is still following the ideas and the requirements that were found years ago. The second issue is that these systems are centralised, which makes them resistant to any changes and vulnerable to system attacks and failures.

The third issue that comes with the current financial systems is that they are exclusionary, meaning that they can deny billions of people access to basic financial tools. Bankers have been able to dodge the creativity that is so critical to the economic progress and vitality. The blockchain can solve all these problems, which is why it is already seen as such an amazing piece of technology.

We have already spent a bit of time talking about the blockchain and how it was initially developed to be the trust factor to help various cryptocurrencies like Bitcoin do well. It is a vast and globally distributed ledger that runs on millions of devices everywhere, and it is responsible for recording anything of value. These things of value include contracts, deeds, titles, bonds, equities, money, and anything that is considered an asset and can be moved and stored peer-to-peer, privately, or securely.

The trust that comes on this network is not from the big banks and governments that have proven to many people that they are not that reliable. Instead, they are trustworthy because of a clever code, cryptography, and a consensus on the whole network. For the first time in history, it is possible for two parties or more, and even those who do not know each other, can make transactions, build up value, and even forge agreements without having to rely on any type of intermediary. In the past, these intermediaries were there to establish trust, to help with record keeping or contracting, or to verify the identities of both parties in the agreement. But with the blockchain, the two parties can trust the network rather than relying on the intermediary.

Given the promise as well as the peril of this disruptive technology, there are many firms in the financial industry, including professional service firms, auditing firms, insurers, and banks, that are starting to take a look at the blockchain and seeing how they can implement it into their own business.

So, what is the driving force that is making these big financial institutions have interest in this technology? There are many of these industries who cite that they like the opportunity to reduce costs and friction in the market. After all, these financial institutions are dealing with some of the same issues that individuals and businesses face, and they are interested in staying up to date with technology to provide better services.

It is possible that the blockchain platform could be able to help many big companies, such as Credit Suisse, Citigroup, Chase, and JPMorgan, to do more with less. It could help them learn how to streamline their business while reducing their risks at the same time. While it is necessary and very advantageous to have this type of viewpoint on the blockchain, it is not always enough to get things done.

The main issue here is how to cut cost from a market or a business that has fundamentally changed. This is where the blockchain can really change the game. By offering these companies a way to reduce their transaction costs for everyone in the economy, this technology will be able to support peer-to-peer mass collaboration that can make many of the organisational forms that we use today redundant.

Let's look at an example of this. Let's consider how new business ventures access growth capital to help it out. In the traditional market, the companies will go after some angel investors during the earliest stages of creating their new business, and then they will move on to venture capitalists and then may work with an IPO on the stock exchange. This type of industry is going to be able to support a few different types of intermediaries, such as auditors, lawyers, exchange operators, and investment bankers.

The blockchain will be able to change up the equation a little bit because it allows a company, no matter what size it is, to be able to raise money in a manner that is more peer-to-peer, thanks to the globally distributed share offerings. This funding mechanism is already making some big changes to the industry of the blockchain.

For example, back in 2016, many blockchain companies were able to raise $400 million through traditional venture investors, and almost $200 million of it went through initial coin offerings, or ICO, rather than IPO. These ICOs are not just new cryptocurrencies that are hiding out and pretending to be companies. They represent various platforms for content or digital rights management. They can also represent distributed venture funds and new platforms that can make it easier for the consumer to invest in ICOs.

The incumbent companies are starting to take notice of the big changes that are coming with this industry and how the blockchain allows companies to raise money in ways that were never imagined before. The venture capital firm known as Union Square Ventures started to broaden out its investment strategy so that it was able to purchase those ICOs directly. Then Andressen Horowitz joined in with USV to invest in Polychain Capital, which is a hedge fund that is only going to purchase tokens.

The list can keep on going. Blockchain Capital, which is one of the biggest investors in the industry, recently announced that it is going to start raising money for a new fund that is responsible for issuing tokens by ICO, which is one of the first for the industry and other companies such as the Intercontinental Exchange, NASDAQ, and Goldman Sachs are currently seen as the largest investors into blockchain ventures.

As with any new business model that is taking the industry by storm the way that the blockchain and ICOs have, there are still some risks. As of right now, there is not much regulatory oversight of the market, so investors and individuals need to be careful about what they are doing online. Disclosures and due diligence can be very hard to find, and some of the companies who have jumped on board of this and issued an ICO have ended up going bust in the end.

However, this is something that has started to catch on and while you do need to be careful about the way that you invest and what you are doing on the market, it is likely that this will keep on going. If the ICOs are done properly, they can not only work to improve the efficiency of raising money for companies of any size, but they can help to lower the costs for investors and entrepreneurs, and also help to democratise the participation of individuals in the global markets.

If the blockchain can change things so much in just a year, think of what else it would be able to do if it were given more time. It is believed that this 'blockchain technology' would be able to upend many complex intermediate functions inside the industry and change the way that we do business. Some of the things that the blockchain would be able to change in this industry include moving value, storing value, trading value, risk and insurance management, identity and reputation, and tax and audit functions.

As you can see, there are many things that the blockchain can assist with and could make them take over the banking and financial industry. But does this mean that we are seeing the end of the banking industry as we know it? This honestly depends on how current financial industries respond to the technology.

The blockchain could easily be used with these financial industries rather than taking them over. It could disrupt things from within while keeping those industries around. The biggest question here is who is going to be the one who will lead the revolution. Moreover, since there are already many big names in the industry who are embracing this technology, it seems that this is something that is going to stick around and really change up the way that we do our banking and other financial work in the future.

And, it looks like those companies who delay in joining this popular trend and figuring out how it is going to work for their industries will be the ones left behind. The 'blockchain technology' may not completely get rid of our current financial industry, but it will certainly change things, and will make it easier to get things done, save, money and even to get loans and other financial services that you may need in life. We are bound to see more of these changes as time goes on.

Could Blockchain Technology Replace Our Financial Institutions Altogether?

With all the different things that you can do with the blockchain technology, you may be curious about whether it is absolutely necessary to have financial institutions at all. Do we really need to have a big bank around that could watch everything that we are doing, interfere if they wanted, or cause other issues in the way that we run our money? Some experts believe that the blockchain technology would be able to replace our financial institutions altogether, allowing us to use and send our money in a manner that we see fit.

While it is certainly possible that the blockchain could take over the financial world and make banks and other financial institutions unnecessary, this is probably going to take many years before we see it. Yes, the blockchain is an amazing technology, but there are not enough people who trust just using this platform for their money. They still want to use their big banks or other financial institutions to help them feel like they can trust the money where it is, and they may not be able to have this trust with the blockchain yet.

Even with this lack of understanding and trust from the general populace, many big financial institutions are starting to use the blockchain to provide better services for their customers. It helps them to get transactions done faster, and it will help lower transaction fees as well.

And since there is one ledger, multiple banks can work together to help provide their customers with the care that they need.

The blockchain was originally released with Bitcoin. The technology was designed to help build trust in the network and to make sure that all transactions that occurred on the network would be accounted for. As the Bitcoin network started to grow and was used more around the world, it didn't take long before people noticed the amazing things that the blockchain technology could do and they started to think of all the other ways that the blockchain could be used.

For those who have only started using a cryptocurrency and don't understand what the blockchain is, this platform may look like an accounting tool. They see that it is a way to hold onto the transactions that happen on the Bitcoin network, but they may not see all the ways that this platform can be expanded out.

The biggest industry that could see some improvements with the help of the blockchain is the finance industry. And since the finance industry works with currencies and in the same manner as we see with cryptocurrencies, it is not going to take too much time or effort to develop platforms that most companies in this industry would be able to use. The blockchain has already been shown to process information faster than other ledgers in the finance industry, and it can help with various niches of the finance industry including payments, settlements, stock trading, and currency transfer.

With the finance industry, many customers are noticing that the process of transferring anything of value is taking forever, especially when you compare how long it takes to complete the transaction itself. Depending on where you would like to get the money to go, it could easily take a week or more to get this money moved. This becomes even more of an issue for those who are trying to send money to another country because now you must worry about extra fees, regulations in each country, and so much more.

But when you are working with the blockchain ledger, you do not have to wait as long to see things happen. The blockchain does not care where in the world each party lives because it can just get it all done on the same ledger. It takes the same amount of time to complete a transaction overseas as it would to complete one right next door. The blockchain can also do this for a lot less money than traditional banks can. All of this comes together to provide a fantastic way for the financial industry to better serve their customers if they use the technology the right way.

The good news is that you would be able to use the blockchain not only to help with some of your regular banking needs, but also to help with share trading. Getting into the stock market is not an instant process because you have to do the research and pick a good stock, talk with your broker about which stocks you want to go with, and then before you can complete the trade, you must make sure that you can transfer the money from your bank over to the chosen trading account. Now, you can speed this process up a bit by keeping some money placed aside in the trading account, but there is still some delay between picking a stock and purchasing it.

The blockchain would be able to help with some of this. You would be able to use this platform to trade when you want to, rather than when the banks think that it is best. In fact, the blockchain is so efficient at helping with share trading and the stock market that the NASDAQ has already used it.

With the NASDAQ and the blockchain working together, you get to use pre-IPO share trades. This helps the consumer to make transfers of share ownership of private companies between the investors before these shares must be listed on the regular stock exchange. And because this is already being done so efficiently, it is becoming really tempting for other businesses in the finance industry to start implementing it.

You do not have to look far before you see that there are many companies already using this kind of technology to grow their business and it is not just something that is found on the NASDAQ. Some other companies that are working with the blockchain right now (and this is not a comprehensive list at all), include Citibank, Visa, and Capital One. These companies are already out there investing in a blockchain distributed ledger that will help them to complete transactions between the three, speed up the transaction time, and ensure their customers are getting the best service possible.

Of course, this is not the only example of the changes you can see when you look at the blockchain technology. Ripple is another example that you can study to see how this platform works. Ripple is a payment network that is being used to transfer anything of value, whether we are talking about commodities or currencies. There are several financial industries who are looking at Ripple and the technology that it offers because it makes it easier to send out payments in real time, and at a low cost, compared to some of the methods these companies may have used in the past. There are at least fifteen top banks throughout the world who work with Ripple to ensure its growth.

Another thing that has really transformed the financial industry is a company that is known as R3. This is a tech company that is working with twenty-five banks, such as JP Morgan and Wells Fargo, to get them all to work together. All the companies who join this project become known as the R3 consortium. The goals that come with this group is like what is going on with Ripple, but it is a bit different because of the ledger that they are using rather than using Ripple directly. It still helps these big banks to work together and get the results they are looking for.

This is not where the blockchain technology has ended with all that it can do with the finance industry. Another example is the Bank of England. This bank is working to make their own personal database that would utilise the blockchain to make things easier for helping their customers. They are also working to team up with other financial industries in Europe to finish up the technology so that they are better able to serve their customers in the future.

The hope with this is that the Bank of England can use this kind of technology to not only help their customers, but also use it to limit the number of cyber-attacks that come their way while also making transactions faster than ever before. Since there are already a ton of the major banks throughout the world who are trying to do the same thing with the distributed ledgers in the blockchain technology, The Bank of England is hoping that they can use their own system to bring them up to the same level as well.

As you can see, there are quite a few industries in the financial world that are using the blockchain technology to help their companies better serve their customers. There are already several big banks throughout the world who are working to try to add on this technology as a replacement to their own databases to provide the best service, complete transactions faster, and save money for their customers.

Right now, most of this technology is just starting to come out so the research about how well it will do is still unsure. But with the big shift over to the banks and other financial institutions ready to take it on, it is likely that the blockchain will continue to grow into the future. Right now, it looks like many of them are just waiting for the right platform to come out so that they can use it for their own.

There are many ways that the blockchain technology can be used when we are talking about using it in the finance industry. Whether the company is looking to speed up how long it takes to complete a transaction, if they want to save some of the costs of using their own ledger, or they want to ensure that they are able to keep up with the future of technology; they will be able to do all of this with the help of the blockchain platform.

What are the Main Blockchain Pros and Cons?

The blockchain is taking over the world. While cryptocurrencies are growing big as well, many industries are looking at the technology that is behind these currencies and seeing what they can do with it. The blockchain has a simple idea, although it can be a little hard to create, and it is not just cryptocurrencies that can benefit from using it. This chapter is going to look at some of the main benefits and the negatives that come with using the blockchain.

The Benefits of the Blockchain

The first thing that we are going to look at is the benefits of the blockchain. There are quite a few industries who will be able to benefit if they are just able to create, or have someone else create for them, a blockchain in their industry. Some of the industries that will benefit the most from the blockchain include:

- **Transparency:** When a system uses the blockchain tech-nology with it, they are improving their transparency, especially when we compare it to some other common record keeping methods. When there are some changes done on the blockchain ledger, each person on the network will be able to see what changes were done. And when someone starts to add information to the blockchain, you will see that it is impossible to change the past transactions that are already in the ledger at all.

  With the current methods of record keeping that most industries have, something is missing. Someone is easily able to get onto these ledgers and fabricate anything or change any transaction that they want in the database. And often, they can do it, without too much work, without other people on the network having any idea. And when you are looking at some of the larger ledgers out there, this can take a long time, if ever, before someone sees that something is wrong. This is why we see so much fraud in the current system, and most of the time the party responsible gets to walk free.

But if the network uses the blockchain, you can keep the transparency around. All the computers who join the network will belong to the blockchain, and all they need to do is approve of any and all changes that are proposed to the blockchain. Because these computers are located throughout the world, it is pretty much impossible for this fraud to occur. And when transactions happen, they are done in real time so people can catch them quickly. While the blockchain may not be able to prevent fraud completely, it does a much better job than other accounting methods.

- **No need for an intermediary:** With the blockchain, you can get rid of the intermediaries that you are using. You no longer must use someone in between you and the other party in order to finish transactions. This can add a level of privacy to your transactions since you do not have to worry about that third-party telling others about the transaction. You can also save much money because you no longer need to pay that third party to help you. The blockchain can make this happen, while still maintaining the trust that you and the other party need to complete the transaction.

- **Decentralization:** This is one of the most popular things about the blockchain. Unlike the traditional banking system that you are used to where each financial institution will have its own ledger that has to be reconciled, the blockchain is done on a shared ledger. Traditionally, if you use your money in one bank to pay another bank, each of these banks will need to reconcile the money. This is a slow process and can take several days to complete. In our fast-paced and modern online world, this is not acceptable.

With the blockchain, you can speed up this process, without needing the banks to give up their control of the ledger. They would all choose to work with one ledger, which makes the transactions faster between them. There are a few steps that need to happen before all this works. Various financial institutions would have to start working together rather than being competitors and would have to give up their current system of keeping track of transaction for their customers.

- **Can keep your information anonymous:** This one you must be careful with. There are many people who get reckless on these networks because they assume that it is impossible for someone to figure out who they are. While there are steps that you can take to keep your information hidden from others and make it hard for someone to steal your information, if you are not careful, a determined hacker could still figure out who you are.

With that said, there are ways for you to keep your identity hidden when you are on these networks. First, you get the choice of an address to use. This address is like your name on the network and will allow you to send and receive money to your wallet whenever you would like. Make sure that you pick out an address that is easy for you to remember, but that will not give away your identity. It is easy for someone to pick up on your habits and transactions on a network if you use your full name in the address. If you are having trouble figuring out what address name to go with, there are a few address name generator sites you can choose from to help.

One thing to note, if you use Coinbase or one of the other exchange sites, they will often provide you with an address to use. These will often just contain your first and last name. So, if you do any transactions with that address, it will show up your name and makes it easy for someone to trace what you have been doing. To avoid this while using one of these exchange sites, just pick out a wallet of your own and assign a different address to that. Then you can transfer the coins over and use them under the new hidden address.

In the white papers that were released with the start of Bitcoin, it is recommended that you change your address after each transaction. This makes it hard for a hacker to trace your transactions because they have no idea which address is yours. The more you change the address, the harder it becomes to locate you. Most people do not want to come up with a new address all the time, but you should still consider changing it on occasion to keep your information safe. If you use the same address all the time, and you do many transactions on the network, it becomes so much easier for a hacker to trace you down.

Staying anonymous on these networks is getting harder and harder. Not only do you need to worry about hackers getting smarter and trying to figure it out, but governments in many countries are starting to nose around and put strict requirements on these networks. Fearing that people may be doing illegal activities or laundering money, the government in the United States has started to require the exchange sites to collect information about all their users and then report the earnings each year.

Many users of these networks are against these changes, citing that one of the benefits of working with a cryptocurrency that uses the blockchain is that it helps them to stay hidden online. But right now, it seems that this, as well as some other more stringent restrictions, are likely to stick around when it comes to cryptocurrencies.

- **Trust:** The blockchain can build trust in so many ways. Without the trust that the blockchain can bring out, it would be impossible for Bitcoin and some other cryptocurrencies to grow. The reason that this technology is considered so effective is that it has found a way to build up trust between all the parties who are working on the transactions. And the way that the blockchain is set up already allows for this kind of trust. The transparency that is found in the system helps to build up the trust. When you join a network that uses the blockchain, you will be able to start looking at all the transactions that are going on the network. And there is plenty of security on the network to help ensure that the information can't be manipulated or changed, which also helps to ensure that the trust sticks around.

- **Security:** When someone places their data onto the record of the blockchain, whether they choose to do this with titles, currency, or some other type of data, it is impossible to change or alter this data. The blocks that contain this data are now on the blockchain and can be traced all the way back to the original genesis block, making it easy to trace where everything belongs. The fact that this kind of data can't be changed, and that it is able to help connect all the different parts of the chain together helps create a trail. Any user on that system will be able to follow the trail if they feel inclined to do so.

This security is important when you work online. Many users join the blockchain because they are tired of all the fraud that can occur with their traditional financial institutions. While your financial institution can take years to find the fraud and may never get it all figured out, the blockchain makes it almost impossible to commit fraud in the first place since all computers on the network need to agree to changes before, they can occur.

- **Saves you money:** Another reason to enjoy the blockchain is that it saves you money while also speeding up how fast you can get transactions done. You can see the transaction get done within a few minutes, rather than a few days, when you use the blockchain. And since you do not need to deal with a financial institution to help with the transactions, you can save much money on the transaction fees.

- **No central authority:** One thing that most people like about the blockchain is that they do not need to worry about a bank, a financial institution, or a government messing with the money. The blockchain can do all the work that these third parties do, without having to fiddle around, causing inflation or other problems. Cryptocurrencies often run on a mathematical equation. They are set to run a certain way. Many have a set amount of currency that can ever be released, and even those that have unlimited amounts have methods in place to prevent too much inflation over time. Everything is run on this code, so there is no reason to have someone in there tampering with the coins or trying to change things.

In a world where it seems that the government is getting too involved in the money and making big mistakes that are costing most middle-class citizens, it is nice to think that there is a safe and secure method out there that you can use to control your own money. And as more governments mess around with the money, causing higher inflation, or fraud, it is more likely that more and more people will see this as a benefit and will join networks that use the blockchain.

The negatives of the Blockchain

While there are many benefits of relying on the blockchain technology to get things done, there are also a few things that make people shy away from on these kinds of platforms. Some of the negatives that you may encounter when you decide to work with the blockchain technology include:

- **Signature verification:** Each transaction that occurs on the blockchain needs to be signed with a public-private cryptography scheme. This is important because transactions work between the nodes in a peer-to-peer fashion, so their source can't be proven without this. These signatures being generated and verified can be complex and can cause a bottleneck issue in some industries.

- **Consensus mechanisms:** In the blockchain, there is some effort that must be expended to ensure that these nodes reach a consensus. Depending on the mechanism that is used for this, it could include a lot of back and forth communication, or a lot of forks, and the rollbacks that come from this. While it's true that this happens with the centralised databases, it is less likely to cause as many issues when the transactions are processed in one location.

- **Redundancy:** This talks about the total amount of computation that this blockchain requires. It can be a lot of waste in the system. For companies who are trying to reduce their waste, this is not a good thing to deal with.

- **Uncertain regulatory status:** Because most currencies are created and then regulated by national governments, these digital currencies can face issues if the regulations by local governments remains unsettled. Many governments are still trying to determine how they are going to react to these digital currencies and the technology that is behind them. Some companies are worried about implementing one because they do not want to put in the time and the money on it, and then find out that their government is not allowing for this technology at all, or is putting really high fees and regulations on using that technology.

- **Large energy consumption:** The cryptocurrency networks must use much energy to validate their transactions, which can take up a huge amount of computer power. This can sometimes be too much for smaller companies to handle, and that is a big reason why it is mostly bigger companies, and often several big companies merged together, who choose to use this technology.

- **Integration concerns:** The blockchain application can offer solutions that will require big changes to or sometimes replacement of an existing system. This can mean a lot of work for the company that wants to use it.

- **Cultural adoption:** The ideas that are behind the blockchain can be difficult to understand, and since they are so different from the traditional methods, it is hard to get companies and individuals to be comfortable with using it.

- **Cost:** While the blockchain can save a ton of money with the costs of individual transactions, the time and the initial startup costs can be huge. Therefore there is a platform like Ethereum, which allow companies to work on their own blockchain platform while still getting paid. This is a great way to invest because it helps the companies to create additional blockchain technology, and since this is such a popular technology right now, it allows for profits.

There are positives and negatives that come with any type of technology that is out there. It is important to see both sides of the picture to understand how they work and to see if an option is as good as the hype. Despite the various negatives that can be said about the blockchain technology, there are still many positives as well, and those positives are big. This is why it is a technology that seems to be growing all the time.

Other Industries That Could Benefit from Using the Blockchain

There are a lot of different industries who would be able to benefit if they decided to use the blockchain. While there are many people who are only familiar with the blockchain in how it works with Bitcoin and other cryptocurrencies, there is so much more that the blockchain is able to do. Almost any industry that needs to save transactions and the information that goes with them can benefit from using the blockchain, if they are able to find a platform that works for them. Let's look at some of the various industries who could benefit from using blockchain to provide better customer service and speed to their customers.

Digital identities

One of the first places where you can use the blockchain is with digital identities. The blockchain is good for this area when the right platform is designed because it will make it easier to know that you can trust the person who is trying to use a specific account. After you get that person set up on the blockchain, that person would then be able to instantly connect with any application that the administrator allows them to use. And they would be able to do all of this without having to use a password or having other measures that are easy to hack into.

The idea of using digital identities is one that is not all that new, but right now they are not that popular because they run into a host of issues. Right now, it is easy for a hacker to set up a fake identity on these systems or for them to steal an identity of someone else. Many of these systems right now will require a password, and these are not always safe. The databases that are responsible for holding onto the password can be hacked any time and it is hard to prevent this from happening. And once a hacker is successful with their hacking, then they can access many passwords to unlock information that they should not have access to in the first place.

The blockchain would be able to help with this issue and get rid of the biggest issues that we find with digital identities. This technology is secure and unique and through several studies, it has been hard to hack through or gain unauthorised access to the information that is inside the account. This blockchain identification system is gaining a ton of popularity, and many companies are working on building similar systems that will work with their business model.

Online voting

Another way that you could use the blockchain is with online voting. If the blockchain is modified so that it will allow for digital signatures as well as for digital identities, then it would become so much easier to authenticate whether a user can be somewhere based on their actions and the other transactions that they do online. To take this a step further, you could then use this technology to help with online voting, and the platform would not need to be changed all that much.

Right now, many countries are running into major issues with voting in general, and this gets worse when they try to move to a digital voting platform. Many people throughout the world do not want to use these platforms because they worry that someone would either be able to see their votes and use it against them or that someone could get on the network and change the votes.

There are some companies who are interested in taking the blockchain and expanding the digital voting capabilities that are there. However, Estonia is the only country that is so far successful. There are some that have tried digital voting on a smaller scale, but it still has a long way to go before it can be all that successful.

This is where we would be able to use the blockchain technology to make digital voting easier to do and much safer. With a blockchain platform, a voter would have the ability to cast their vote and then double check that it had been sent. Their privacy would always be maintained in this system and no one else would be able to see that identity. This system would help more people vote because they could do it without having to try and make it to the polls each election season.

The medical field

One great way to use the blockchain technology is for those who want to see more efficiency within the medical field. When you visit your doctor or another medical facility, you often must spend much time filling out forms, even if they were sent some of your information ahead of time. Since the blockchain is a type of distributed ledger, you get the benefit of when the ledger is changed in one place; it will be updated on every system that has that blockchain.

This is helpful because if you visit a specialist or move to a new doctor or even see someone while on vacation in another state, your doctor will be able to look at the blockchain and see all the medical history that is available about you in one place. For patients who have trouble remembering everything about their medical history, especially the elderly, or those who may have forgotten about a procedure in the past or who don't want to share some information, this could potentially be lifesaving.

There is a lot of potential that can come from using this distributed ledger within the healthcare industry. It is very unlikely that you have seen only one doctor from the time of your birth to when you die. Most people skip around to different doctors based on their age, if they need to see a specialist at any time, if they don't like a doctor, or if they move to a new location. Every time that you go to a new facility, you will need to waste much time filling out paperwork and answering questions to ensure that your medical history is up to date. This gets more time consuming the older you are, and it is also easy to forget a lot of information along the way. And depending on the information that you forget, it could make the doctor's job more difficult to help you.

With the help of this blockchain platform, you will not have to worry so much about remembering each piece of information. The doctor would be able to share the results of your appointment, or surgery, or something else, on the blockchain database. Then, if you do see another doctor for some other reason, such as moving or going to see a specialist, that new doctor can get into this database and see all the records from your past. If each medical facility used this properly, all the records about you from birth to that current moment would be on the blockchain, allowing the doctor to get full information about you and helping you to get the best care possible.

Not only would this be able to save you much time filling out paperwork at the doctor's office, it could even save your life. Let's say that you end up going on vacation and get admitted to the emergency room. Rather than hoping that you are doing well enough to remember your medical history, the doctor would be able to go to your health records and see what part of the issue may be. They could also see other possible complications, such as a latex allergy which would be important if you needed emergency surgery.

For a patient who has been in to see various doctors over the course of a few years, this database can be helpful as well. The patient may have a variety of complaints that do not seem related when they see individual doctors about them over a few years. It is sometimes hard to get in to see your primary care doctor when you are not feeling good, so you may see various doctors in the same facility, or you may skip around. But if a doctor was able to look at all these different visits, they may be able to put the pieces of all these illnesses together and diagnose you right away.

The medical field could greatly improve with the help of the blockchain technology because it would put much information right into the hands of your doctor when they need to take care of you. It could save most patients some worry and time when they are heading to meet a new doctor, and you would often end up with better patient care because the doctor is sure that they are seeing your whole medical history.

Insurance

You can also see that the insurance industry would be able to benefit from the blockchain technology as well. We will spend some time talking about smart contracts later, but these are a big part of helping insurance companies out because these contracts allow for two parties to get into an agreement without dealing with a third party or the fees that are associated with these other parties.

With a smart contract, you and the insurance company could add in the information that was needed regarding what requirements there are for the insurance policy, who owns the policy, and so one. And then whenever the conditions of that agreements are met, the contract will go through and self-execute. In terms of the insurance company, if you have a policy and want to claim something on it, such as an accident in your car or something gets broken on your home during a storm, you would read the agreement in the smart contract, submit the required information, and if it meets the criteria in the contract, then the contract would send you the money for the repairs.

It is common for many people to avoid dealing with an insurance agency, especially when it comes to claims. And when there are emergencies, such as after a big storm, it is sometimes hard to get a hold of these agents because they are busy talking to everyone. But, with the help of these smart contracts that are done on the blockchain, you can cut out the insurance agency and still get the money that you need for the claim.

Music

This is one that you may not think about that much with the blockchain, but the world of music could also use this technology to make things better. Many musicians struggle with pirating and other issues that make it hard for them to get paid, especially when they put their music on a streaming service. These musicians want to be able to get their royalties, but with promotions and other services, some streaming sites are struggling with figuring out what they should pay the artists.

One company in the music industry which is starting to use this 'blockchain technology' to help with royalty payments is Spotify. This company is using a platform of the blockchain that was developed by the company known as Mediachain, to ensure that their payment structure is transparent to any artist who uses their sites.

Rentals, properties, and other real estate agreements

These smart contracts are really a cool thing to use, and there are many industries that will be able to benefit from using them. Even working with rentals, real estate, and land sales can be done with the help of a smart contract rather than relying on a third party to come in and do the work. You also save some of the costs that come with traditional real estate exchanges.

In the past, when you wanted to move into a new apartment, buy or sell some property, or do something else in real estate, you would need to work with several people at a time. This would include various lawyers to draw up the contracts, a real estate agent to list your property or to find a new one, the title company, and more depending on the transaction.

With the help of the blockchain technology, you could use these smart contracts to get the common tasks done instead of relying on the third parties. You and the other party in the agreement would just need to find a real estate smart contract and then add in some personal information to determine who each party is. When the conditions are met for this contract, the contract will be able to go through and release the payment, the information, or the other thing of value that both parties agreed to.

These smart contracts are good for both parties because they help each other trust the other party without knowing them. It also saves both parties a lot of money because they do not need to trust someone else to come into the transaction. However, with the blockchain platform and the help of these smart contracts, you will know that the transaction is safe and secure for both parties as well.

What are the Truths Behind Many Blockchain Myths?

While many people may have heard about the blockchain in the past because they have worked with Bitcoin or one of the other cryptocurrencies, most may be confused about how the blockchain really works. They are not able to describe exactly what it does, and because of this, it is easy to believe some big myths that come out about the blockchain. This chapter is going to look at some of the myths that are out there about the blockchain and discover the truth about this neat piece of technology.

The first myth that you may notice with the blockchain is that most people think that it is the same as Bitcoin. Since Bitcoin has been around for some time and was released at the same time as blockchain, many people end up getting the two mixed up. Bitcoin is a network that utilises the blockchain in order to keep track of all the transactions that go on in the Bitcoin network. Bitcoin would not be able to function without the blockchain technology, but there are many ways to use the blockchain without using Bitcoin.

The blockchain is going to enable peer-to-peer transactions, to be recorded on a ledger throughout the Bitcoin network. However, Bitcoin is the cryptocurrency that two people can exchange with each other without them having to go through a third party, such as a bank.

Also, many people believe that the only way that you would be able to use blockchain is in relation to cryptocurrency. While cryptocurrencies frequently use the blockchain to help them work, the blockchain is able to work well all on its own. There are a ton of ways that you can use the blockchain, and with some modifications, it is possible that almost all industries and businesses would be able to use the technology that comes with the blockchain.

Some people believe that the information that happens on the blockchain and its activity is not publicly available. The majority of what happens on the blockchain is easy to trace, contrary to what most people think. Additionally, the blockchain does not have a lot of hidden secrets, and there is not much dark criminology that comes with the activities that are on it. Anyone can check out the blockchain if they join the network, which is free to do, and you can see what activity is going on.

Many people believe that all the transactions that they do with Bitcoin and other cryptocurrencies are going to be anonymous. Bitcoin will use a public ledger that will track what was sent from one address on the network on to the other. While you can choose your address and keep changing it so that it is harder to trace you, someone can still go on and see what transactions are occurring on the network. This helps to keep some of the transparency that is needed on the network. Many government organisations are working to establish some relationships with the major exchanges to help complete out a map of the address to the owner so that no one can use these digital currencies, such as Bitcoin, to hide money from the government.

While many cryptocurrencies are volatile, it does not mean that the blockchain technology is the thing to blame and that it is unreliable. This is a misconception that occurs from those who associate the volatility of these currencies with how credible the technology of the blockchain can be. Blockchain has many applications that expand out beyond cryptocurrencies, and in the long term, it is going to be a big game changer. As with many early technologies, the initial use cases, content, and interfaces are overrated, but the technology that helps to run them are underrated.

There are also many people who may not join these networks because they feel that these currencies are only used for criminals to hide their activity. It is true that anonymity and decentralisation are nice features that can be used by criminals. However, these are also good features that law-abiding citizens who are in politically or economically unstable environment can use. If you are not able to trust the banks in your region because of corruption or if you are worried about how your currency could destabilize soon, then it is best to keep your money in cryptocurrency instead.

Another misconception is that the blockchain is seen as a storage mechanism. This is an advantage that comes from using the exchange, but it is not all. The transactions that occur with the help of the blockchain are going to happen between two people, rather than the coins just staying put.

Some people believe that these currencies are only for people who are financial or technology nerds. But, the blockchain is used in cryptocurrencies that can be enjoyed by anyone and everyone. The average consumer may want to shy away, but you will find that with just a little bit of work, it will not take long before you learn how to use the currency for your own needs.

Some people also do not understand how the tokens and coins are different. The coins are going to have one use, to act as a simple store of value, while tokens are used to store complex levels of value such as fungibility, income, utility, and property. The property that you use can be transactions for real estate and for intellectual property. However, when talking about tokens, these can capture commodities or loyalty points.

And finally, many people think that cryptocurrency is going to be greatly different from some of the other currencies that you will use. There has been a lot of hype around the blockchain as well as some of the crypto aspects of cryptocurrency. But, the question that you need to ask yourself is what is fundamental about any currency that you will use.

Basically, a currency of any type, is going to be a unit of measure as well as a way that we can communicate value. What asset forms the backbone of the value for any new cryptocurrency that comes out on the market? These coins may not be printable and usable in some of your favourite stores right now, but you are still able to use them to buy and sell products or send and receive money through that network. This shows that the currency is not that different from what you are used to with traditional currencies.

As these digital currencies start to grow and become more popular, it is likely that more of these myths are going to start fading away. Most people do not understand how they work because these currencies are relatively new, and a lot of people have never given them a try. But, these currencies are easy to use, and the blockchain is the driving force that provides the security and ease of use that is needed to make these currencies run.

What are the Blockchain's Main Application Scenarios?

The Blockchain is going to be so important when it comes to making sure that Bitcoin and the other cryptocurrencies work. However, the things that the blockchain can do is going to be completely independent of Bitcoin. This means that you will be able to get a lot of the benefits that come with the blockchain without having to be on the Bitcoin network.

From a functional standpoint, the blockchain is going to provide the foundation to enable a secure, trusted, and decentralised data exchange. Because it focuses on solving a highly complex problem, the developers of this technology have been able to create capabilities that are so important to many applications.

There are many ways that you can use the blockchain as an application. Some of the ways that you can do this include:

Decentralized IOT

The internet of things, IOT, is becoming a big trend when it comes to software for modern enterprises. While many of these platforms are going to be focused on a centralised model where the hub control or the broker of the interaction between the devices tries to keep them going. However, this model is not very practical for many different scenarios in which the devices need to exchange data between themselves autonomously.

The blockchain is important in this because it provides the foundational capability of decentralised IOT platforms. This can include record keeping and secured and trusted exchanges of data. With this IOT architecture, the blockchain can serve as a general ledger that will work to keep a trusted record of the messages that are exchanged between the IOT topology and smart devices.

Keyless signature

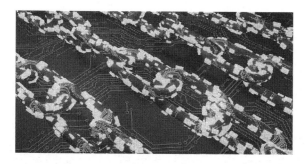

A public key infrastructure, which is also known as PKI, is one of the fundamental technologies that have been around to help power the signatures of data. These PKI models are going to rely on a central authority to stamp and then validate signatures that are on a data payload.

Thanks to some of the characteristics of the blockchain, you can work with PKI a bit more and overcome some of the limitations that have occurred. This happens because you are able to work with a KSI; a 'keyless security infrastructure'. This KSI model will work with 'cryptography' that is a hash function, which will allow the verification to rely just on these hash functions as well as the availability of the blockchain ledger to let you onto the sites that you would like.

Proof of Possession

Another issue that a lot of our current technology has trouble with is being able to validate the possession or existence of signed documents. You want to make sure that the right person signed a document and that it is legally binding in a contract. The challenge that comes with traditional documents when you need to validate them is that they rely on a central authority to store and then validate these documents. This can present you with some big security challenges, and this is much harder to do, the older the documents are.

With the help of the blockchain, you are given an alternative model to 'proof of existence' as well as possession of legal documents. When you leverage the blockchain, a user can store the timestamp and signature associated with a document inside the blockchain. It can then use this information to validate it at any point.

Security trade settlement

The CSD, or Central Security Depositories, has been a very big part of our modern bond and equity trading process. The centralised nature of these is important to make sure that these trades are as successful as possible. However, this settlement process using the CSDs can be slow and expensive, and each trade settlement is going to take about two to three days before it is done.

The blockchain can provide you with an interesting alternative to using the CSDs as a decentralised ledger. This is because this ledger can keep records of any transaction that occurs without having to stick with that central authority. The query capabilities that come with the blockchain make it easier for the trades to be settled in just a few minutes, and sometimes in a few seconds. Also, using the blockchain for this work can help the transactions get done at a fraction of what you would spend with the current solutions using CSD.

Anti-counterfeiting

Counterfeiting is a big issue and challenge when it comes to modern commerce. Segments like electronics, pharmaceuticals, and luxury goods are constantly going to be affected by this issue. Unfortunately, the solutions that are on the market will require you to trust a third party, which can cause some friction between both the consumers and the merchants when completing the transaction.

Because the blockchain is secure and decentralised, it enables you a good alternative to using the regular platforms to avoid counterfeiting. It is possible to envision a model where marketplace, merchants, and brands are part of the blockchain network with some nodes that can store information that helps you to validate all the authenticity of various products. The brands do not have to worry about trusting a central authority with the authenticity information and then you can rely on the decentralised trust models and the security of the blockchain to know that counterfeiting does not occur.

Ethereum Explained

Ethereum is another type of cryptocurrency you can work with. It is a bit different compared to Bitcoin, so if you have used that currency in the past, you may be a bit confused about why Ethereum is not working the same way. Ethereum is a great cryptocurrency on its own, but many users do not understand the differences between it and Bitcoin.

However, Ethereum and other cryptocurrencies work in a slightly different way. This is a decentralised system that is not controlled by anyone, much less one central authority. It does not have one point of failure. It is run from thousands of computers of people who volunteer, which means that it is pretty much impossible for it to go offline. Plus, your personal information will stay on your computer, while other content can still be under your control without having to obey the rules that are imposed by various hosting services like YouTube.

A second thing to enjoy with Ethereum is that even though Bitcoin and Ethereum are compared to each other, they are different from each other and they have some big goals that are different. Bitcoin is one of the first cryptocurrencies and a money transfer system. It is also built on and supported by a public ledger that is called the blockchain.

Ethereum is a bit different. Ethereum took the blockchain technology that is behind Bitcoin and then helped to expand what it can do. It is a whole network, with its own internet browser, payment system, and coding language. Even more important, it will enable the user to create their own decentralised applications with the help of the blockchain that is present on the Ethereum platform.

The applications that the individual is able to make can either be completely new ideas or reworks of concepts that are already in existence. This is going to be helpful because it cuts out an intermediary and can cut out the expenses that are associated with having a third party involved in it. For example, if you worked with Ethereum and created a decentralised version of Kickstarter, you will not just be getting an artefact for your contribution to the company, you would have the ability to receive some of the future profits of that company. In addition, applications that are based on Ethereum will be able to remove all sorts of payments to third parties for these services.

As we mentioned a little bit before, Ethereum is considered a decentralised system, which means that it goes with more of a peer-to-peer approach. The users taking part of it, supports each interaction that happens and, there is no central authority involved in the whole system.

Instead, this whole system is going to be supported by a global system of nodes. These nodes are going to be volunteers who can download the entire blockchain to their computers so that they can completely enforce the consensus rules of the system, which helps to keep the network honest. And, when the nodes are successful with this, they will receive some rewards for the work.

Several different consensus rules are present, and these, along with some other parts of the network, are going to be dictated by smart contracts. These smart contracts are going to be designed to perform transactions, as well as some other actions, within the network with some parties you may not know all that well and may not trust. The terms that both parties need to stick with will be added into the contract. Then the completion of these terms will move on to trigger a transaction or other specific action that you and the other party agreed on ahead of time.

These smart contracts are nice because it helps both parties to trust each other without having to trust or pay for a third party to help them get it all done. Many people who have used these contracts believe that these are a part of the future and will soon replace all other types of contractual agreements. These contracts provide a lot of security and are much faster and less expensive than some of the other options that you have.

Who created Ethereum?

So, now that we have taken some time to explore Ethereum a little bit, it is time to look at how this cryptocurrency got started and a bit more about why this is such an important currency to know about. In 2013, Vitalkik Buterin described the idea he had for Ethereum in a white paper. He sent this out to several of his friends, who ended up sending it on to more. As a result, there were around 30 people who liked the idea and went so far as to talk to Vitalik about his concept.

This project was announced in January 2014 with a core team that was meant to help get it up and going. In just a few months, the team decided to have a crowdsale for Ether, which is the token for Ethereum, to help fund their development of the currency.

Is this considered a cryptocurrency?

For the most part, Ethereum is going to be more of a software platform that works to act as a decentralised internet and app store. A system like this one will need currency to pay for all the resources that are needed to run any program or application that is done on Ethereum. This is where the Ether that we talked about before comes into play.

Ether is the digital bearer asset for Ethereum, and it is hard to get started with Ethereum without this token. It does not require another party to come in to process payments at all. However, it doesn't really operate just as a digital currency. It also acts as fuel for the decentralised apps that are on the network. If the user would like to go through and make some changes in one of the apps that are on Ethereum, they will then need to pay a transaction fee to help the program properly process this change.

The transaction fees will be calculated based on how much work that action requires. The amount is also going to be calculated based on the computing power that is needed for the action and how long it takes to run this application.

How are Ethereum and Bitcoin the same?

Many people are confused by how Bitcoin and Ethereum are similar. They do have a similarity in that they are cryptocurrency, but they are very different types of projects with different goals. While Bitcoin has worked to establish itself as a stable and successful currency, Ethereum is a multipurpose platform with its currency Ether just being something that helps the smart contracts work, rather than being a way to make purchases or send and receive money.

How does Ethereum Work?

The platform of Ethereum is going to work on the blockchain, but there are some tweaks to it that makes it work a bit differently than you would see with Bitcoin and some other cryptocurrencies. The blockchain that is used for Ethereum is described more as a machine for transactions. When it comes to using computer science, the machine is going to be capable of reading a series of inputs and then transitioning to a new state based on the inputs it is given. Then when these transactions are executed, that machine will then be able to move over to a new state.

Each of these states for Ethereum will oversee millions of transactions. These are then going to be grouped to make some blocks, with each of them being chained together into one of the previous blocks. However, before these are all added into the ledger, there needs to be validation process, and this will happen during the mining process.

While we will talk about mining a little bit more, later in this book, the mining process in Ethereum is going to be when a group of nodes will apply some of their computing power in order to complete a challenge for proof of work. This is basically a mathematical puzzle. The more powerful a computer is, the faster it will be able to go through and solve that puzzle. The answer that it comes up with for the puzzle is a proof of work and can help to validate the block.

Many miners are competing to create and then validate these blocks. This is because when the miner is able to do this process, they will generate some more Ether and then they will receive these as their reward. These miners are so important to making sure that the Ethereum network is going to work because they not only make sure to confirm and then validate transactions and other operations that happen in the network, but they make sure that there are new tokens that are added into the network.

What can I use Ethereum for?

The first thing that you can do with Ethereum is to build and deploy various decentralised applications. Also, any type of centralised service can be altered to decentralised with the help of the platform that Ethereum can provide. The potential of Ethereum platform for building apps is not limited by anything other than the creativity of the creator.

The technology that comes with the blockchain on Ethereum has the potential to change how web-based services and industries can be used. For example, when we are looking at the insurance industry, you could take the money that is placed in life insurance and redistribute it fairly as well as transparently with the help of the blockchain. And then with the help of the smart contracts, the clients will be able to submit their insurance claim, doing it all online, and then receive an automatic payout right away, if the claim meets the requirements that they agreed on with the company.

Basically, the blockchain that comes with Ethereum is able to bring efficiency, trust, security, and transparency, to any kind of industry. It can also be used for DAO, (Decentralized Autonomous Organizations), which will operate completely independent and transparent of any intervention and without a single leader. These are run by programming code and can work with smart contracts that are written on the blockchain. These DAOs will be owned by people who purchased the Ether tokens. However, the number of these tokens that you purchase will not equate to equity shares or ownership. Rather, these tokens will provide you with some voting rights.

The Ethereum network is a little bit different compared to some of the other digital currencies that you may come to use. While Bitcoin is all about being a payment system that allows you to send and receive money and make purchases online, Ethereum is going to rely on helping to support various applications on the blockchain. You will need to use the Ether to make these applications run and work properly, but you would not be able to go through and purchase other products.

Litecoin Explained

There are a lot of different cryptocurrencies that you can choose to go with. While many people like to use Bitcoin or Ethereum because they are so well-known, there are other options that you can choose that are just as effective and may even help you to earn more money. One of the cryptocurrencies that you may want to consider when entering the market is the coin Litecoin.

To start, Litecoin is a peer-to-peer cryptocurrency as well as an open sourced software project. It has some similarities to Bitcoin, so if you have used that currency in the past, this one is easy to work with as well. Creating and transfer of these coins will be based on an open source protocol with cryptography, rather than being controlled by a central authority. Moreover, while it is like Bitcoin, you will find that Litecoin is much cheaper and way faster than its predecessor.

In December of 2017, Litecoin had finally reached a new high of $360.93. This is much lower than what Bitcoin has seen (at one time it got almost to $20,000), but compared to where Litecoin was the year before, at $4.40) this means that the coin has risen by 8200%. This is reflective of how the market for cryptocurrency has grown as well, with an increase in the total market being more than 3600%.

Many people like to compare Litecoin to Bitcoin. They function in much the same manner, and you will be able to use Litecoin to make purchases or to send and receive money. However, there are some differences. The transaction fees are much lower when you work with Litecoin, and the pricing of Litecoin is more rational compared to Bitcoin, which would make it perform well even in the future.

As more stores begin to accept these digital currencies, it is likely that Litecoin will see a bigger increase as well. It should not be long before you can purchase anything you would like, from clothes, groceries, jewelry, and electronics with Litecoin or some of the other digital currencies. And since the value of this currency is determined by its current demand on trading websites like Coinbase, GDAX, and Bitfinex, it is likely that there could someday be a shopping platform that allows the price of products to change constantly so that they reflect the value of the coins that the seller accepts.

In addition to being able to trade and purchase Litecoin, you can also decide to mine it. This is a technical activity, as we will discuss later, and you will need to have a good computer as well as quite a bit computer knowledge to help you get started. Add in some good processing units that can rapidly solve the equations for mining, and the process becomes easier for you to complete.

Trading Litecoin

While Litecoin is not as popular as Bitcoin and does not have the value that Bitcoin does right now, it is still an extremely popular option to go with when you are ready to mine your coins. The rise in how popular Litecoin and other digital currencies are is due to the demand for alternative currency options that can keep themselves separate from governments and centralized banks.

There is also a good deal of demand from investors and traders who have begun to realize that these cryptocurrencies have a huge potential for profit. Therefore forex traders and other investors have been able to change the way the market works. Compared to other forms of investing, cryptocurrencies are much easier to join and millions of traders, both beginners, and more seasoned traders have gotten into the market to buy and sell coins.

There are a few different options that you can go with when it comes to trading Litecoin or other cryptocurrencies. One method is 'day trading'. With day trading, you will need to watch the market and determine where the market value is. This is usually somewhere in the middle of where the prices fall over for several days. Then, while watching the market, you will purchase the coins when the price goes below this market value. As soon as the amount goes back up and gets to or above market value, then you sell the coins.

You may not make a ton of money off each trade with day trading, but it can help you to earn something. And when you do a bunch of these trades, your income will go up a lot. Remember that with day trading, you must purchase and then sell those coins on the same day. Holding onto them for longer fits into another type of trading and it uses different strategies for success.

Many people like to work with the buy and hold strategy. If you would like to earn some good money with Litecoin and other cryptocurrencies and you don't want to do a ton of work watching the market like a hawk, and waiting a while to get the money, then the buy and hold strategy is the best one for you.

With this strategy, you will purchase the Litecoin that you want to use, and then leave them in a secure wallet. Then, over a few months or even a few years, you will hold onto those coins, doing nothing with them. After a certain amount of time has passed, you will then trade them out for a larger amount. With Litecoin, you may have purchased the coins for $4.40 a year ago, but now they are worth more than $360. You could trade the coins out now and keep that profit for yourself.

Using Litecoin as a tool worldwide

Litecoin is like other types of digital currency in that you can use them anywhere, and anyone who has an internet connection is also able to use them. The fees that you get with Litecoin are much lower than what you would see with a bank transfer or a credit card company, so this can save you a lot of time and money.

An example of how this can help you is; let's assume a person living in France wants to send out a payment to someone who lives all the way in China in just a few seconds while ensuring that both parties will receive a proof that the transaction occurred. Litecoin has been designed to enable these cheap and quick payments, and the process is as simple as sending out an email to a friend.

More about Litecoin

Because of how Litecoin was designed, there can only be 84 million Litecoin ever released, and right now about 55.58 million of them have been mined or released already. This means that more than 30 million coins are still available for miners to mine. This figure is based on the idea that Bitcoin had a limit of 21 million coins and that Litecoin was made to be four times faster than Bitcoin.

The whole point of having a fixed amount of coins means that you will not have to worry about inflation messing with the overall value of the currency, like what happens with the Euro or the Dollar. For any forex trader who feels that there could be an issue with a currency dropping in value, they can purchase Litecoin and then hold onto that investment before selling it back over to their currency later, hopefully with the ability to make a profit.

Also, many people like to work with Litecoin because it does not have the external influence of the government. Many times, traditional currency can be influenced by the government and with quantitative easing and inflation, it is hard to keep up with the value of the money. But with Litecoin, there is no governing body that can do this, which makes Litecoin more sustainable in the long term.

Litecoin was first introduced in October 2011 and was created by Charlie Lee. Lee was a former employee with Google, and he designed Litecoin to be a complement of Bitcoin while also solving some of the common issues that had been found with Bitcoin at the time. Lee was able to look at the core code from Bitcoin and make his modifications to the protocol so that it would now be easier to allow large-scale adoption of the currency.

A big goal that came with Litecoin when it started was that it needed to reduce the block confirmation timings down from 10 minutes to 2.5 minutes, allowing more transactions to be confirmed at a time. This helps Litecoin to be faster than its predecessor and for each 2.5 minutes, there is another twenty-five Litecoin that are generated. This helps to keep Litecoin growing at a steady rate and solves the problem of Bitcoin being too slow for some users.

Litecoin still has a ton of room for growth, wide adoption in the cryptocurrency market, and potential uses. Right now, it is a good idea to watch which companies are going to start adopting and accepting Litecoin to help with the various transactions they do. Once more companies start to accept Litecoin as a form of payment, it is bound to grow so much more in the future.

What are the Alternative Blockchains?

While we know that many benefits come with using the blockchain, there are actually a few alternatives coming out that can be amazing to use as well. The Blockchain Technology was one of the first of its kind, being there to help startup Bitcoin and get these digital currencies going. It was fast, it could send and receive money from anywhere in the world, and there was the benefit of having a system that was secure as well as transparent all at the same time.

While there is a lot to love about the blockchain, there are also some issues that have come to light in recent years about the blockchain. Due to some of the newer coins and the alternative blockchains that are out there, the older version of the blockchain sometimes is seen as outdated. Let's look at some of the different alternative blockchains that you can use, and which may already be on some of the cryptocurrencies that you are comfortable with using.

Distributed ledger

One option that is sometimes used instead of a blockchain is known as a distributed ledger. With this ledger, you do not need to work on a chain to store the information, which can save time and some of the hard work of the miners. This distributed ledger is going to focus on the idea of sharing the database amongst all the participants who are working on the network. With the blockchain, you only focus on how the data was stored and linked with the other data in a chronological manner inside the blocks. You can imagine which one makes more sense and works the best.

With the blockchain, you must include an algorithm for consensus, but this is not that important when you are working with a distributed ledger. And one of the major problems that has come up with Bitcoin and other digital currencies that uses the blockchain is that they were not easily scalable with this method. With the distributed ledger, you theoretically have better options when it comes to scaling.

Hedera hash graph

This is a new platform that is meant to provide a new form of a distributed consensus. This is a new way for people all over the world, people who do not even know each other, to start collaborating and doing transactions online without needing to have an intermediary there at all. This platform may be new, but it is really secure, fast, and fair and also, since it is different from some of the popular blockchain based platforms that you may have used in the past, it is not going to require a proof of work system that will be hard on the computer and hard to keep up with.

The Hedera Hashanah Council is known as the counseling body of this network. It consists of 39 leading organizations and other enterprises in their fields, and the membership is meant to reflect the variety of geographies and industries which use this platform. These members oversee electing a governing board while also giving their expertise when needed. This governing system is set up to ensure that not one person will be able to have all the control over the system or that a smaller group of the members can have more influence over the governing body as a whole.

Ceptr

Another option that can be used and is starting to grow in popularity is known as Ceptr. There are a lot of different parts that you will enjoy when it comes to using Ceptr and some good ways to describe it include:

- A framework that is used for distributed applications in a cooperative fashion.
- A quantum leap in large-scale collective social intelligence.
- A platform that is peer-to-peer and is used to build up some new Commons.
- The protocols for this are pluggable so that you can let everything talk to everything on the network.

- It has an architecture that is organically organised.

The main point of working with Ceptr is that it is a global nervous system that makes working with others and sharing information or your currency easier than ever. Right now, it is a nonprofit organization that does not have much money, but some platforms and groups can help newcomers learn more about this chain and how to invest or use it for themselves.

Smart Contracts Explained: The Truth

Another thing that you can work with inside the blockchain is a smart contract. These smart contracts are neat and have been used by many parties who want to come up with an agreement together, but who do not want to be stuck paying for a third-party to help them out. These smart contracts can help with real estate transactions, rental properties, and even with insurance, wills, and more.

A smart contract is basically a self-executing contract found on the blockchain. Both parties will be able to put in their information to the smart contract and then when both conditions are met, then the contract will go through the conditions and close itself out. It is secure for both parties and helps to save them some time and money.

With traditional contracts, there can be much hassle. You first need to pay someone else to come in with the contract and watch you sign it. You and the other party could pay thousands of dollars to make these contracts, and all the other person does is hand you the document to sign and agree to. Also, depending on what you have in the contract, bringing in a third party could risk the privacy of either party.

This is not an issue with a smart contract. It is as secure as a regular contract, which is a benefit to both parties, and it can execute the terms of the agreement all on its own. Moreover, since you do not need to bring in some third party to help you out, you can save time, money, and maintain your privacy all at the same time.

Let's look at an example of how this smart contract can work. Remember that both parties are going to benefit from this type of contract, so it is worth your time to consider using it. For this example, let's say that there is a landlord who is wanting to rent out an apartment, and there is a tenant who would like to rent that apartment.

Now, the landlord wants to hold a deposit before the tenant moves in. This helps the landlord to make sure that the potential tenant is serious about moving in and can protect them in case there are some issues with the apartment later. Most of the time the landlord will request the deposit before setting up a background check and agreeing to let the tenant move in.

On the other hand, the tenant may want to move into the apartment buildings, but they may be worried about handing over to a landlord they do not know. They may think that the landlord will just run off with their money or something else will happen before the background check clears.

This is part of the benefit of using a smart contract. Both parties can go in and sign the contract, putting in the information that they want into it. They can agree that there is a deposit of a certain amount that needs to be placed before the landlord can begin doing a background check to rent out the property. Once the tenant places the money in for that, the landlord will have some days to do the background check and other things required before renting out the room.

Now, if the landlord finishes the background check and presents a key to the tenant on the date listed in the contract, the smart contract will release the money for the deposit over to the landlord. However, if there is some reason that the landlord is not able to finish the work on time or they decide that they do not want the tenant to live in their apartment for some reason, then the deposit money, which has been placed in escrow at this time, will be returned to the tenant.

As you can see, this can help to protect both parties. The landlord can see that the deposit money is in place before they do the background check and see if the person is right to live there. But if the landlord doesn't think that the tenant is a good fit or just does not respond for a few days, then the tenant will get their money back.

Are smart contracts legally binding contracts?

One question that many people have about these smart contracts is whether they are legally binding or not. Technically, code cannot be law, so these contracts have traditionally not been allowed to be legally binding. If someone backs out of a contract, it is very hard to get anyone to pay attention and do anything about it. But in August 2017, the Enterprise Ethereum Alliances have been working to change this status.

Right now, it seems to depend on the state you live in whether a smart contract is a legally binding document or not. In March 2018, Tennessee enacted a law that started to recognize signatures on the blockchain and smart contracts as legally binding documents. According to the new law with smart contracts, "no contract relating to a transaction shall be denied legal effect, validity, or enforceability solely because that contract contains a smart contract term in it."

There are several other states in addition to Tennessee that have adopted the same idea when it comes to whether these smart contracts can be legally binding. Notably, Colorado, New York, Florida, Nebraska, and Wyoming are joining this state to expand out the legality of blockchain and its technologies and how they are used in a legal way and for their use in the government as well at this time.

If you do decide to go with a smart contract, it is important to realize that it is not necessarily legally binding. Both parties have to agree to this, and if one of the parties does not and ends up running away, it can be hard for you to find someone who will step in and help you out since you did not use a legally binding contract. There are many benefits to using these smart contracts, but unless both parties are committed to keeping with the terms, it is hard to enforce that contract.

The blockchain technology is doing wonders to change the way that we do business and how we sign contracts, make money, send and receive money and so much more. These smart contracts are just another example of some of the cool things that you can do when it comes to the blockchain technology.

Mining Explained: Do we need it?

The process of mining is important when it comes to working with cryptocurrencies like Bitcoin and Ethereum, but it is one that is not really understood all that well. It is complicated to do, and many times people will not want to waste time and resources to do the work. But without the miners, the blockchain would not be safe and effective, and then no one would want to participate in these networks. Let's look at how mining works and why it is so important to make sure that these currencies work well.

For some cryptocurrencies, there are only so many of the coins in existence at a time. The makers of these coins did not want to release all the tokens at once to ensure that they could keep up with demand and keep the supply low to provide more value later. However, there needs to be a way to let these coins out and get them in the market as more people start to use the network.

Also, the reason that people choose to work with these networks is because of the blockchain. They know that these blockchain ledgers are open so they can check these out, but that their personal information is safe, as well as the information about their transactions, so that a hacker or someone else is not able to come in and steal that information. If the blockchain did not work this way, it would be hard to convince anyone to use these digital currencies.

So, how does this all tie into mining? Miners are the ones who create the unique codes that protect your information on the blockchain. Using their computer and some good programming skills, they will create a code that keeps your block of the blockchain secure while also getting it to match up with all the other blocks that came before it. When the miners are successful, they will receive a reward of the token they are working in, which effectively releases more of that token into the network.

When you are done with a block, and it is filled up with all the transactions that it can hold, that block is sent over to a miner. They can then get to work on creating a unique code for that block using the information that is inside the code, and sometimes bringing in other information if needed and if that new information doesn't mess with the transactions that are present.

These codes need to have a few parts to them. First, they need to be random so that they are hard to guess. They also need to have a specific number of zeroes at the front, which will depend on which cryptocurrency you want to work with. And finally, all the characters need to be dependent on each other. That way, if one of the characters is ever changed by a hacker or someone else who is trying to get into the network, then it will mess with everything. And when this happens, it will not take long, even for a beginner, to see that something has happened in the code.

In addition, all the characters in the specific block are dependent on each other, also, the characters in that one block will match up with the whole blockchain as well. This is another security measure so that your information is safe. No one will be able to go in and try to tamper with the blockchain or any of the information inside without everyone on the network finding out.

This is all a competition. The block will be available to any miner who wants to work on it, but the miner who can get it done the fastest is the one who will get the reward. This can mean that you will spend much time working on these codes and never earning something. Working in a mining pool or getting some good software could be the solution that you need to this issue.

Once the unique code is done and accepted, it will join the main blockchain for the whole network. Anyone will be able to go and look at this at any time, which helps to provide transparency for the network, but the unique codes make it hard for people to get your personal information and use it how they want. There is also no longer an issue with someone trying to hide their information or trying to take money out of the system without everyone noticing.

Of course, this takes up a lot of computer power and time, and the work gets harder the more people who are in the network. So, in the beginning, you may be able to get the codes done faster, but the reward is usually smaller so you will not earn as much. As the currency grows and is around for a longer period, the end reward may be more, but it is a lot harder, and can cost more in computer software and power, to earn a reward. Either way, as soon as you come up with a code that is accepted and approved, you will earn a reward and can use it however you want in the network.

There are a few things that you will need in order to make the mining process work. You need a good computer that has a lot of power behind it and can hold much memory. You will need some software around to help you go through the process for you to save some time. Also, you will need a space to keep your computer and a wallet to store the coins if you are successful to get the reward.

Because of the challenges that come with mining these currencies, many people decide to join a mining pool. In these, a group of people will work on the same code, each person working on a different part, and since they share the work, they will share the rewards. You may not make as much in one shot with this method, but you can earn a steadier income this way compared to doing it all on your own.

While the mining process may seem complicated and like it will take up much time, it is important to maintaining the security and the safety of these digital currencies. Without it, many users would choose not to use the blockchain or the currency because they would worry about someone tinkering with the transactions or stealing their personal information. Miners get the important job of setting up the codes that help the blockchain stay secure while earning a nice reward that can be put back in the network to help it to keep growing.

ICO Explained

An ICO, or Initial Coin Offering, is a method of fundraising in which new projects will be able to sell their underlying tokens in exchange for either Ether or Bitcoin. It is sometimes compared to the IPO, or Initial Public Offering, where investors can purchase shares of a company.

The idea of ICO is new, but it is a very big topic of discussion when it comes to the blockchain community. Many are worried about ICO projects because these are often unregulated and could allow their founders to earn an unjustified amount of capital in the process. On the other hand, others argue that it is an innovation in the traditional venture-funding model.

To help determine how ICOs will do in the future, the U.S. Securities and Exchange Commission has decided on how these tokens will be issued in the now infamous DAO ICO, which was the catalyst to force other projects and other investors to look again at the funding models of many ICOs. The most important criteria that stands out with these ICOs is whether the token can pass the Howey Test. If the token does not pass this test, then it needs to be treated like a security, and it can be subjected to various restrictions while it is on the SEC.

So, what is the Howey Test? This is a test that was agreed upon by the Supreme Court in 1946 to help determine whether a transaction is going to qualify as an investment contract. If the transaction does not, then it is considered a security and needs to be subject to certain registration and disclosure requirements.

When using the Howey Test, the transaction is going to be considered an investment if:

- It is considered an investment of money
- There is an expectation of profits from this investment when you start
- The money that you invest is inside a common enterprise

- The profit that you get comes from a third party or a promoter.

Although this test will use the term money, some of the later cases have expanded to include some assets other than money. This isn't necessarily defined, and each court is going to have different interpretations. For the most part, a federal court is going to define this kind of common enterprise as one that is horizontal, or where investors will pool their money and their assets together to help invest a project.

These ICOs are easier to structure thanks to the ERC20 Token Standard, which will help the developmental process become more efficient. Most of them will work by having the investor send funds, which is usually in the form of Bitcoin and Ether, using a smart contract that will store the funds and then distribute that value in a new token at the agreed date.

There are not many restrictions on who can participate in these ICOs, if the token is not seen as a security. And since you are using money from a bigger pool of investors, the amount that is raised with these can be huge. One big issue that comes with these ICOs is that most of them are going to raise money as a pre-product. This means that all your investment is going to be speculative, and therefore, risky.

History of the ICO

There were originally several projects that used the crowdsale model to fund their work in 2013. Ripple is a good example of a digital currency that pre-mined one billion XRP tokens and then sold them to investors who were willing to exchange either Bitcoin or fiat currencies for the Ripple. Ethereum is another example who was able to raise more than $18 million in 2014 and was the largest of these ICOs that were done at that time.

This soon expanded out more. The DAO was one of the first attempts at fundraising for a new token on Ethereum. The promise with this was to create a decentralized organization that would be able to fund other projects on the blockchain. However, it was still unique in that the token holders would take the governance decisions.

This project was able to raise money, making over $150 million, unfortunately a hacker was able to get onto the system and drain out millions from the organization due to some issues with the system being vulnerable. After this happened, the Ethereum Foundation decided to go with a hard fork, which allowed them to claw back the stolen funds.

Although this first attempt at using the ICO on Ethereum ended up failing, the developers of blockchain realized that working with the Ethereum token was easier than going through other methods to get their funding. Pre-product companies were able to raise a ton of money, more than they were able to before, and in a short amount of time, the company Aragon was able to raise $25 million in fifteen minutes while Basic Attention Token raised $35 million in 30 seconds.

Are these ICOs legal?

This is a hard question to answer. Legally, these ICOs have existed in what is known as a gray area because arguments are made for and against them. The SEC's decision has been able to clear up some of the gray area so that investors know what they are getting into. In some cases, the token is used simply as a utility, which means that it allows the owner to access specific protocols or networks. If this is the case, it is not seen as a security. However, if the token is used as an equity token, or that it is used to appreciate in value, then it is considered a security to use on the exchange.

While it is common for many investors to purchase tokens to access the platform that is associated with it later in the future, it is very difficult to refute the idea that most purchases for the tokens will be for investing in the future. This is easy to ascertain given the fact that many of these projects have not released a commercial product.

These ICOs provide a way for startup tokens to get the money that they need to create their own platform sometime in the future. The investor puts their money in, either as fiat currency or Bitcoin or Ether, and then the developers will have the money that they need to get started. These investments are speculative because the creators are trying to sell the idea that their tokens will do well in the future, and that can be a hard thing to predict.

How Can I Invest and Make Money with the Blockchain Right Now?

There are many reasons why people like to use digital currencies. They like that the blockchain keeps their information safe and secure. They may like that they can send and receive payments from across the world with no fees and hardly any waiting time, thanks to the blockchain. And, some like that they can remain anonymous and do transactions without the government getting involved or knowing who they are online.

However, one major reason that people are looking at the blockchain, as well as the currencies that are run on it, is that they want to be able to invest their money and earn a profit in the process. These currencies and their blockchain are gaining much popularity, and you will be able to use that to your advantage to make some money in the process. There are many ways that you can invest and make money inside the blockchain technology which includes the following:

Invest in a blockchain platform

Many people choose to invest in a blockchain platform because they are not entirely sure how the blockchain works or what steps they must take to make one of their own. This is a safe alternative that allows someone else to do the work while still making them some money in the process. Many companies want to create various blockchain platforms, but most requires funding to get this done. You can provide them with some of the funding and then earn that and a certain amount or percentage back as well, when the company completes and sells their platform.

The best place to look when planning to invest in the blockchain technology is the Ethereum currency. This currency was specifically set up to help with creating more blockchain platforms because it offers an open-sourced version of the blockchain that anyone can use. This is the best place to get started with this technology, and it will help you to find a company that is the best investment for you.

Create a smart contract

Creating a smart contract can be a good way to make money with the help of Blockchain technology. We talked about these smart contracts a bit earlier on, but basically they are contracts that are found on the blockchain and will self-execute when each party meets the conditions. They are safe and effective for each party to use and they get the benefit of not having to rely on a third party to sign the agreement and that it can save them some money.

But, before these two parties can sign a smart contract, they need to have a contract to work with. If you have some technical knowledge, you can create some of these contracts and offer them for sale to those who need them. You can create ones that are for specific needs, such as real estate or insurance, or you can create ones that are blank and let the users fill them out as needed.

You will then be able to charge a small amount for the parties to use your smart contract. This puts some money in your pocket, and it's still much less expensive than what the other parties would pay a professional to do the work. They get a discount, they get privacy, and you get a paycheck out of it.

Create your own blockchain

Many companies have decided to create their own blockchain and sell it to other industries who may use it. Blockchain has so many uses, from helping the banking industry work on transactions faster to ensuring that reservations are placed properly, that insurance claims can be filed faster, and so much more. However, for these industries to do all this work, a blockchain needs to be developed first.

Creating a blockchain is not an easy endeavor. Usually, a company will work with many individuals to put it all together properly, and when it is done, you either earn a paycheck each week for your work, or you can earn some of the profits when the project is sold.

Angel funding and startup ventures

The idea of angel funding is not a new one. One variation that is gaining a lot of popularity though is the idea that you should invest in a startup that uses the blockchain technology as its foundation. As the Bitcoin network grows and becomes more popular and even more accepted by mainstream businesses, the number of entrepreneurs who are interested in working with and experimenting with this technology will climb.

But, working with the blockchain in this manner can have some issues. First, you need to have some funding to get started. Providing the startup with the funding that they need can help you to get in on the ground floor of a company that could be the next big thing. However, you must consider that there is a risk of doing this and there is no guarantee that the money you invest will return with profits. You must do your research and find out which startups will be the best and safest for your investing needs.

Altcoin crowdfunding

Crowdfunding is a popular as well as a mainstream method for helping raise seed capital for many types of investments. If you want to get yourself involved with Blockchain technology, one option that you should consider is a method that will rely on these alternative coins. When you are using this method, the total coin supply will have been mined out right at the start, and then these are sold out during the ICO, prior to this network being officially launched.

There are many companies you can use to do this, but Bitshares is one of the best to choose when you are getting started. There are quite a few apps and services that run on Blockchain technology that has been able to utilize the pre-sale method to help them raise the right funds. When using this method, the investor is going to be given a chance to purchase these coins, relying on higher expectations, meaning that when the price of the coin goes up, you will be able to make money.

Penny stocks on the blockchain

You may have heard about penny stocks a bit if you ever took the time to invest in other areas. It is even possible to use penny stocks inside cryptocurrency as well. You can work with Bitcoin to make this happen, but other digital currencies can work as well, such as Altcoins and Litecoin.

Over the past few years, there have been a few alternative digital currencies developed in an attempt to give Bitcoin some competition, but they did this not by being the same as Bitcoin, but by having a design that allowed them to fill in the needs that Bitcoin was not able to meet. For example, some of these currencies were developed to enable digital asset registry, providing increased privacy to their users, and even to allow an escrow service, just to name a few. And, with several of them, you will be able to go through and invest in penny stocks.

Stockpile Bitcoin

This method is like what you see when investors take advantage of stockpiling gold when they think that the price is going to rise. You go in and stockpile Bitcoin a bit with the idea that the price of these coins will go up. These two assets have a lot of things different about themselves, but they have many of the same investment principles.

Basically, both come down to the idea of supply and demand. When there is a limited amount of supply and the demand increases at the same time, the value is going to increase. However, if the supply stays the same or goes up, and the demand starts to decrease, then the price will go down.

So, with this method, if you feel that the supply of Bitcoin is going to be limited compared to the amount of demand that it will have soon, then you would go in and stockpile the Bitcoin as much as you could afford. Then, when the price goes up, you will exchange the Bitcoin back out for your fiat currency and keep the change in the process.

Day trading

Day trading can take much time and will require a good amount of knowledge about the market and how cryptocurrencies work. You will also need to spend a good deal of time on your computer watching the market and making your moves. Most trades with day trading will not yield a big amount of money in the end, but if you do a bunch of these throughout the week, and you end up being successful with it, you could see some big profits over the long-term.

With day trading, you will use the blockchain to make purchases of a coin sometime during the day. Then later during that day, you will sell the coin and try to make a profit. You must be good at watching the charts for that coin and understanding how the market works. You must look and see what the market value of the coins is for that day. Then, when you see that the price of the coins is below that market value, you will purchase it and hold onto the coin for a little bit.

As you continue to watch the market, you will wait to see when the coin reaches market value or goes above market value. Then you need to sell the coin back and keep the profits. The lower you can purchase the coin for and the higher you can sell it for, the more money you will make. All this needs to be done within the same day though. It doesn't matter if it takes just a few minutes for the trades to happen or all day, just if you do the purchasing and the selling all in the same day.

Since the cryptocurrency market is open 24 hours a day due to being open in all parts of the world, it is tempting to get started with day trading and then hold onto a position overnight if it is not going well. This then turns into swing trading, which requires some different strategies. You are not necessarily able to control what happens when you are asleep and if you keep your money in the trade overnight, you could easily lose a ton of money and have no way to stop it or get out of the market until you wake up the next day.

Another thing to consider when you do day trading is how much it is going to cost for all the transactions. Each time that you transfer your traditional money into the chosen currency and then transfer it back out again, the exchange site is going to charge you a little bit of money. It is not all that much, but it can add up if you are doing a bunch of these transactions, so it is something to consider. Make sure to factor it into your costs when you investigate day trading so that you ensure that you earn money on as many of your trades as you possibly can.

The buy and hold strategy

This is probably one of the most popular trading strategies out there. It is simple to use and is perfect for beginners, and there have been many people who have made it rich doing this. You just need to watch the market on an occasional basis, rather than having to watch it all the time, and you need to have some startup cash to get into the market, and then you are good to go.

For this method, you should watch the market and find out when your chosen currency is at a low point. Then you exchange your traditional currency for the chosen cryptocurrency and you just keep the money in the network for some time, usually between a few months to a few years depending on how the market is doing and how much money you would like to make.

This is a very long-term investment strategy. If you want to move the money around a lot or make a ton of money right away, then this is not suitable. If you would like a method that is simple, does not require a bunch of work, and will not require you to watch all the daily ups and downs of the market, then this is the strategy for you. You just put your money in and let it stay there until the market goes up.

There are many examples of investors doing well with this, but let's look at Bitcoin. In February of 2017, the value of the Bitcoin was about $2500. Let's keep it simple and say you bought one Bitcoin at this time. The value of the bitcoin has slowly gone up, but it hit a spike in December of 2017, reaching almost $20,000 in value during that month. If you had exchanged your one Bitcoin back out for traditional currency during this time, you could have made almost $17,500 per Bitcoin that you owned.

Even if you missed out and held onto your coin too long and it went down, there is still a profit to be made. In May of 2018, the price of Bitcoin was hovering around $9000, so it is still a profit from $2500. Moreover, if you joined the market back when Bitcoin was just starting, you could have purchased the coins for a few dollars and seen that grow to that almost $20,000 point by now. And of course, the more of these coins you purchase, the more profit you can make while the market does well.

However, you do need to watch the market for cryptocurrencies and see how they are going. If you had joined the market back in December 2017, you would have a coin that is now worth half its value, and it may never get back up to the value it was before, meaning that you would lose money on this.

If you do go into the buy and hold strategy, make sure that you pick out a good wallet. It is usually not the best idea to go with an online wallet because these are not all that secure and hackers would love nothing else than to get your coins while they sit there. Since you will most likely keep your coins in place for at least a few months or more, then you should consider going with cold storage. This takes the key of your coins completely offline and makes it almost impossible for anyone to get a hold of the information and take your coins.

As you can see, there are many ways that you can use the blockchain technology to make money. Some of the methods will be more speculative in nature than others, which can make them riskier to some investors. It is important to research the method of investing that you want to use ahead of time so you understand how they work as well as how much risk you could be taking when you choose one of them. While these digital currencies are growing like crazy, there is still much risk that comes with them and understanding how they work can keep your money safe.

How to Spot Scams

With the rise in popularity of cryptocurrency, many scams are popping up. Hackers and other scam artists alike are seeing the potential of working on these networks. Many people are eager to join a network, they may not pay that much attention to what they are doing, and the scammer could take the money and run without any way for the user to find them again.

If you want to invest in cryptocurrency, you must watch out for scams. Falling for these can cost you thousands of dollars, and there is no way to get the money back. Some of the red flags to watch for when signing up with a new cryptocurrency include:

- Being promised a commission if you sign others up along with you.
- Being promised that upsell memberships are going to alleviate the high fees that are required to withdraw your money from the account.
- You are on the network, but you are not allowed to use your machinery to mine that currency.
- Finding out that a government, even if it is not your own, has branded that particular cryptocurrency a pyramid or Ponzi scheme.

Always do your research before signing up for a new cryptocurrency to make sure that it is legitimate and stick with the well-known exchange sites. Many beginners have lost money because they went with an exchange site that promised low fees for exchanging, and then the scammers just ran off with the money without exchanging it for a cryptocurrency. As usual, if a deal sounds too good to be true, then it most likely is.

Appendix A: Terms to Know

Many of the terms used in this guidebook are technical or programming terms. Those who have spent some time learning computer science may already know these terms, but many who are curious about the blockchain technology have no interest in computer programming. Understanding what the terms of the blockchain mean can help you navigate through cryptocurrency easier than ever.

Some of the other terms that you should know when navigating this new world include:

- **Address:** In cryptocurrencies, addresses are long strings using characters to send, hold, and receive money. To confirm a transaction, the owner of a Bitcoin wallet has two encrypted keys, a public, and a private key. The wallet address is going to be public, but the private key is needed to verify with the system that your digital signature is confirmed and that the transaction is legal.

- **Altcoins:** These are any cryptocurrencies that are not Bitcoin. Could include some options like Ethereum, Litecoin, and Ripple.

- **ASIC:** This stands for application specific integrated circuit. It is basically a chip that has been designed to do one task. For Bitcoin, the ASIC's are intended to solve hashing questions to help mine new Bitcoins.

- **Bitcoin:** Bitcoin was the first successful cryptocurrency on the market and is currently one of the most popular. It relies on peer-to-peer transactions and the blockchain to send and receive money no matter the location of the other person.

- **Block:** A transaction that occurs on the blockchain will combine into a single block. Every ten minutes a new block that is about 1 MB is made. Every block has four parts including a timestamp, a way to reference the previous block, information about the transactions inside, and Proof of Work that shows how the block is secure.

- **Block explorer:** This is a tool that you can use to explore the blockchain that is present in a specific cryptocurrency. This can provide you some information on the coin supply, transaction growth, and hash rate.

- **Block reward:** This is the number of tokens that the miner will get for processing a transaction in a block. These are used to encourage miners to mine, hence keeping the security up on the network.
- **Chain linking:** This is a term that is used to connect two separate blockchains together. It will allow for transactions to occur between the two chains.

- **Client:** The client is going to be a software program that a user can execute on their mobile device, laptop, or computer to launch an application.

- **Cloud mining:** Classic mining of cryptocurrencies will require someone to invest a lot of hardware and electricity to the system. Cloud mining companies make the mining process more accessible to everyone. A user can get onto the website, invest some of their money in a company with mining datacenters, and hopefully make a profit. The company will manage the money and then use to invest in more mining equipment. As an investor, you will get a share of revenue, but not as much as you could with traditional mining.

- **Consortium blockchain:** These are blockchains where the consent process will be determined by a set of nodes that are preselected.

- **Cryptocurrency:** Cryptocurrency is like cash or money. The biggest difference here is that cryptocurrency is digital. The first one on the market was Bitcoin, but there are more than 1000 cryptocurrencies on the market.

- **Crypto jacking:** This is a stealthy use of your computer to mine cryptocurrency. The first effort to do this was on Piratebay. This website allowed an in-browser mining software so that if someone came and used the website, then the computer started mining the cryptocurrency using that browser. There are several other attempts for this. The best way to discover if a device is mining cryptocurrency is to look at the task manager to see if there is any weird CPU performance.

- **Decentralized Application (dApp):** For an application to be decentralized, there are a few criteria that must be met which includes:

- The application needs to be open-sourced and can function alone without a government taking over control. The program is also able to adjust the protocol to react based on market response and suggested enhancements, but all the users must agree to these changes.

- The information, as well as the operation records, need to be stored with cryptography on a blockchain that is public, without the possibility of a failure point.

- Cryptographic tokens are used on these systems for admission to the application and can include input of value from the miners.

- The application produces tokens that go with a standard algorithm that will act as proof of value.

- **Decentralized Autonomous Organization:** These are organizations that will run without any type of human involvement and are under the control of some business rules that are incorruptible. These rules are applied to be auditable publicly, and they are managed across the systems of each investor. People will be stakeholders by purchasing some stock in the organization, and this helps them to earn a share of the profits or decide how it is run.

- **Digital signature:** These are used to sign for some of the transactions on the blockchain. Any time that the blockchain has a transaction added to it, it is going to be signed using the private key of the user. Then this transaction is sent over the network using the public key. The miners will be able to verify the signature based on what the public key is.

- **Double spending:** This will happen when an individual can spend the same money more than once. Bitcoin was able to implement a solution for this in 2009 by verifying all the transactions on the blockchain.

- **Encryption:** This is the action of securing your data in a way that is only readable with a code or a password. It helps to protect the information that is exchanged.

- **Forks:** The strength of the blockchain is going to rely on how democratic the blockchain is. Everything is considered decentralized, and all the parties will have access to the same information. However, there is going to be a weakness if everyone needs to approve changes but can't due to lack of consensus with the network, this then is what leads to a fork. A fork is going to happen when part of the network wants to make changes, but the other part doesn't.

- **Genesis:** This is the very first block in a new blockchain platform.

- **Halving:** This is the decrease in how much payment the miners can earn after a certain number of blocks have been mined. For Bitcoin, the amount is going to split after 210,000 blocks, but each cryptocurrency is different.

- **Hash:** Miners need to take a look at blocks that are in the blockchain and validate them. To do this, they will add a password or a type of digital fingerprint, which is known as a hash. This is a unique identifier and can't be repeated.

- **ICOs:** These are Initial Coin Offerings, and they are like the financing of the company. The company will offer tokens rather than shares, and then the shareholders can pay using their coins.

- **InterPlanetary File System (IPFS):** This is a peer-to-peer program that will connect the computers with the exact system of records. In some ways, it is similar to the Internet, but it is more of a way to swap data on the blockchain. To keep it simple, it offers a lot of data which is a content-addressable, block storage model that will have addressed links. This will help to build up a data assembly where you can build versioned filed system and blockchains.

- **Lightning Network:** This is a type of decentralized network that will rely on smart contracts so that payments can be instantly done across all the users in the network. It can help transactions on the Bitcoin network to occur right away without having to wait for confirmation times on the block. This allows for millions of these transactions to occur in seconds, with low costs.

- **Merkle Tree:** This is a data structure in which every piece of information you have is linked to another. You can link them with the help of a hash. The content will be used to determine what the hash should be. By using this hash, the content is addressed and then considered indisputable because if someone tries to change the information, the hash is going to change, and then the connections will be altered. Each block will point to the block that was ahead of it and if you change the block, the hash will change and will make your block invalid.

- **Miners and digital mining:** The act of mining is the process of working to find coins through the creation of chained blocks based on the timing that is set in the protocol. The miners will use some powerful computers that will check to see if the transactions are performed right. The miners will add on the hash, or the digital key, for each of your blocks.

- **Mining pool:** In a mining pool, users can come together to share computing power. If a coin is created from the shared work, then the users will receive a portion based on how much they helped out with the equation.

- **Node:** The node is going to be a computer that is a part of the blockchain network. If you join the Bitcoin network, then your computer becomes a node.

- **Oracles:** An oracle provides a link between the outside world and the smart contract. It provides the information needed by the smart contract so that it can execute.

- **Private blockchains:** This is a type of blockchain where the permissions to use it will be left for one single institution.

- **Private key:** When you open up a cryptocurrency wallet, you will receive a private and a public key. The private key is a number that allows you to make transactions on that blockchain. It will be stored locally and is secret. You can also print it out if you choose, so that it is not seen on your computer. The private key is necessary to mark the operation, but the wallet will do this automatically for you.

- **Proof of authority:** This is the consent tool in the private blockchain that will allow the client to use their private key to make the blocks on the blockchain.

- **Proof of work:** POW is a requirement that shows support for a transaction. They exist to allow for a trustless agreement. For example, a hashed block is considered a POW.

- **Ring signature:** This is technology that will provide you some anonymity on the blockchain. They will ensure that the output of a transaction is traceable. Messages that are signed with the ring signature are going to be endorsed by someone or a group of people. However, no one will be able to tell who in the group created that signature.

- **Sidechains:** These are blockchains that are interoperable with one another. This can help avoid market fluctuations, fraud, security breaches, fragmentation, and more issues. These allow digital assets and tokens from one blockchain to be utilized in another blockchain and then move back if needed without issues.

- **Smart contract:** These are digital agreements that are placed on the blockchain. Once both parties sign them, they can't be altered.

- **Tokens:** These are the chips that are used in cryptocurrencies to purchase a good or service. This could include the Bitcoin or Ether on those networks.

Conclusion

No one can predict the future however it does seem increasingly likely that blockchain technology has too many advantages to not be utilized on a grand scale for future transactions. Given time, social confidence will grow, and more businesses and financial institutions are sure to get on board and enjoy the added efficiency and cost savings which blockchain technology offers.

From an investment point of view, anyone who wishes to can get involved with cryptocurrency investment however one needs to be cautious in the same way as you would with any other investment portfolio, perhaps even more so. This book has taught you what you need to know to get started but it is still essential to continually keep up to speed with the latest developments and find out what is still relevant in this fast-paced technology. At the end of the day it's your money and your call so take your time, choose wisely and of course never put all your eggs in one basket or think you know for a fact where the market is headed. If you do choose to invest, my initial advice would be to start small and never invest with money which you can't afford to lose.

I wish you the very best of luck with whatever path you choose.

I'd like to thank you for taking the time to read my book. I really do hope that you enjoyed it and that it's given you real value.

If you would be so kind as to leave an honest review, I would very much appreciate it.

Thank you.

Arthur T. Brooks.

Made in the USA
San Bernardino,
CA